TRAINING THE YOUNG HORSE

TRAINING THE YOUNG HORSE

Vanessa Britton

B.T. Batsford Ltd · London

For Darryl; a mere youngster himself.

First published 1994

Typeset by Servis Filmsetting Ltd, Manchester and printed in Great Britain by Butler and Tanner, Frome, Somerset

Published by
B.T. Batsford Ltd
4 Fitzhardinge Street
London W1H 0AH

A CIP catalogue record for this book is available from the British Library

ISBN 0 7134 7183 2

CONTENTS

ACKNOWLEDGEMENTS

My very grateful thanks go to Christine Dunnett of College Farm Stud, Hingham, for her help with photo sessions, where the horses used were literally being handled, bitted, rugged, etc., for the first time as the photographs were being taken.

To Sue Vincent, of Willow End Equestrian Centre, for help with lungeing photo sessions, where my own three-year-old horse was used.

Also to show producer Wendy King, for allowing me to photograph her youngsters while they were being lunged, long-reined and backed, and who puts up with me pouncing on her for many other photos at frequent intervals!

I am, as always, indebted to my husband Derek, who supports me in everything I do. Without him, horses would not be trained, photographs would not be taken and books would not be written!

All photographs are by the author, and all line drawings are by Carole Vincer.

FOREWORD

In the current age of Do-It-Yourself, it is all too tempting to include horses in this category, which, to the unitiated, could be fraught with danger and open to abuse. In dealing with animals, no book can ever be a substitute for practical experience, but Vanessa Britton has produced a very realistic approach to the problems of handling and training, explaining in great depth the whys and wherefores from the very first stages through to more advanced work. She lays particular stress on the importance of the earliest days in formative years and how this relates to problems that arise much later in life.

Much can be learnt from this book; the author writes from practical experience and love of her subject and it should have a wide audience among all ages, covering many of the pitfalls that could be avoided by the aspiring owner/trainer. The training programmes are well planned, progressive and clearly defined, and I can recommend it to all who wish to enjoy the pleasure and satisfaction of training their own horses.

Jane Wykeham-Musgrave, B.H.S.
1994

INTRODUCTION

Deciding to train a youngster, perhaps from foal onwards, is an enormous undertaking. If you are successful, the feeling of satisfaction will be immense. If something goes wrong, however, the horse that you have tried to educate will carry the problem with him for the rest of his life.

Many people come across a time in their involvement with horses when they need to handle and perhaps train a young horse, yet the guidance available is limited, and they often find that they are left to cope alone **(1)**.

If you are such a person, and have perhaps come across this situation because you have taken on employment after recently gaining equestrian qualifications, or simply because you have decided to acquire and train an unspoiled youngster of your own, this book aims to give you a structured guide from which to work.

Your aim when educating the young horse will be to produce a sensible, well-balanced and willing animal which has faith in you. He should be confident in all that is asked of him, and, through correct management in his early years, should not be allowed to believe that he can take advantage of you.

A horse which is well-educated as a youngster will always be of use, even if he is not destined for stardom. The horse which has been spoiled through incorrect management, on the other hand, is likely to be passed around from owner to owner, abused because no one can handle him.

Correct early education lays a sound foundation from which a horse will develop further. You can only bring out what natural abilities the horse may have, and should not, therefore, set out with a preconceived idea of producing a show jumper or a dressage horse. Although hints to a horse's future will be given out during his early education, his full potential will only be determined by further education in specific areas.

It is to this aim that this book is designed. We will take the uneducated youngster and carefully develop his mind, temperament and body, through a structured process, to ensure that he maintains soundness and health throughout his all-round education.

It is impossible to put a limit on the length of time that such education will take, as every horse needs to be treated as an individual. Patience will be rewarded, however, for the feeling that you will receive when you first hack your horse out on your own will be one of contentment, satisfaction and pride – a sensation hard to better.

We are constantly told through the equestrian media that the inexperienced should never attempt to train a young horse. I maintain that it is not so much inexperience but lack of knowledge that is the real problem. How can someone gain experience in an activity if they are never allowed to try it? For this reason, the motto of this book is: acquire the knowledge, by reading and watching experienced trainers, and then proceed – with caution – to gain the experience.

Many people who set out to train a youngster often become disillusioned when they start to read up on the subject. 'Only use an indoor school', and 'Never try to do things on your own', are pieces of advice often given as 'law', but few people training their own horse, or those who want to learn how to do it, have such facilities and help available to them.

An indoor school and plenty of help are indeed the 'ideal' for training youngsters, but it is perfectly possible to manage with the help and facilities that you have at your disposal. This book does not assume that you are training your youngster in an 'ideal' situation, and therefore concentrates on how to train him safely with whatever means are available.

The traditional term for taking an unridden horse and turning him into a horse accustomed to having a rider on his back is *breaking*. This term is somewhat unfortunate, however, and should not be taken literally. We do not aim to *break* a horse in spirit or body, to a point at which, because he is so weak, he succumbs to our demands, which enables us to ride him.

In recent times, due to the influence of American trainer Monty Roberts, who '*starts*' his horses in a uniquely American way (see pages 116–17), the word *starting* has been used, instead of *breaking*. Our aim is to start the horse correctly, in preparation for further training, and so it is here that we will break with tradition and, for the rest of this book, the term starting will be used in preference to breaking.

1 Many people are so disillusioned by seeing spoiled horses pass through their hands that they decide to breed a foal and train it themselves

Part 1

PRE-TRAINING

1
FIRST THINGS FIRST

To buy or breed?

Beginning with the right horse is of paramount importance, for the job of re-training wayward animals is not one to be taken lightly, even by the most experienced horseperson. An animal has to be acquired which is basically sound in mind and body. This means that he should be good-tempered in all respects, and have good conformation. He does not need to be the *perfect* horse, for there are very few of those – if any – to be found. Certain minor faults can therefore be overlooked, as long as you are aware of them and are prepared to account for them in the horse's training.

Although the horse may have been handled (and the older he is the more he *should* have been handled), if no-one has attempted to back him, he would be described as *unspoilt*. In order to acquire an unspoilt horse, there are two options open to you: either to buy, or breed. This decision is a matter of personal choice, and will depend on your own circumstances. There are certain drawbacks to both methods, and neither one is a guarantee of finishing up with a horse which suits you.

If you do not have your own mare, or do not feel confident in breeding from your mare, you will obviously be looking to buy a horse. If you set out to buy an unspoiled youngster, you will be able to see what you are getting in terms of conformation **(2)**. You will also be able to satisfy yourself regarding the horse's temperament by seeing and handling him prior to purchase. You cannot be sure of his history, however, as, although the previous owner may assure you that nothing untoward has happened to him, unfortunately owners who wish to sell horses cannot always be believed.

If you decide to breed, remember that there are no guarantees as to how a home-bred foal will turn out. Your mare may have good conformation and a good temperament, but it does not necessarily follow that the foal will have the same, although choosing a compatible stallion will obviously enhance your chances of breeding an animal suitable for your purpose. At least with such an animal you will be sure of its history, which is extremely valuable when training your own horse.

If you have bred your own horse, you will be starting his education from birth. By starting with so young an animal, you will, with correct management, be able to instill confidence and understanding from the beginning, which will help immensely when it comes to training sessions.

It is also possible to buy a foal while he is still with his dam, and, as long as you are satisfied that he will be handled and looked after correctly, there is no reason why you should not do so **(3)**. When he is weaned, at about six months of age, he will still be young enough to enable you to mould him to your ways.

Buying a weanling, which, as the name suggests, is a foal just weaned up until its first birthday, needs consideration. It is a time in a horse's life for great change: not only will he be separated from his dam, but he will also feel strange in a new environment. A weanling needs a companion of some sort, and, although a small pony

2 This unbacked three-year-old, in excellent health, is ready to start her training

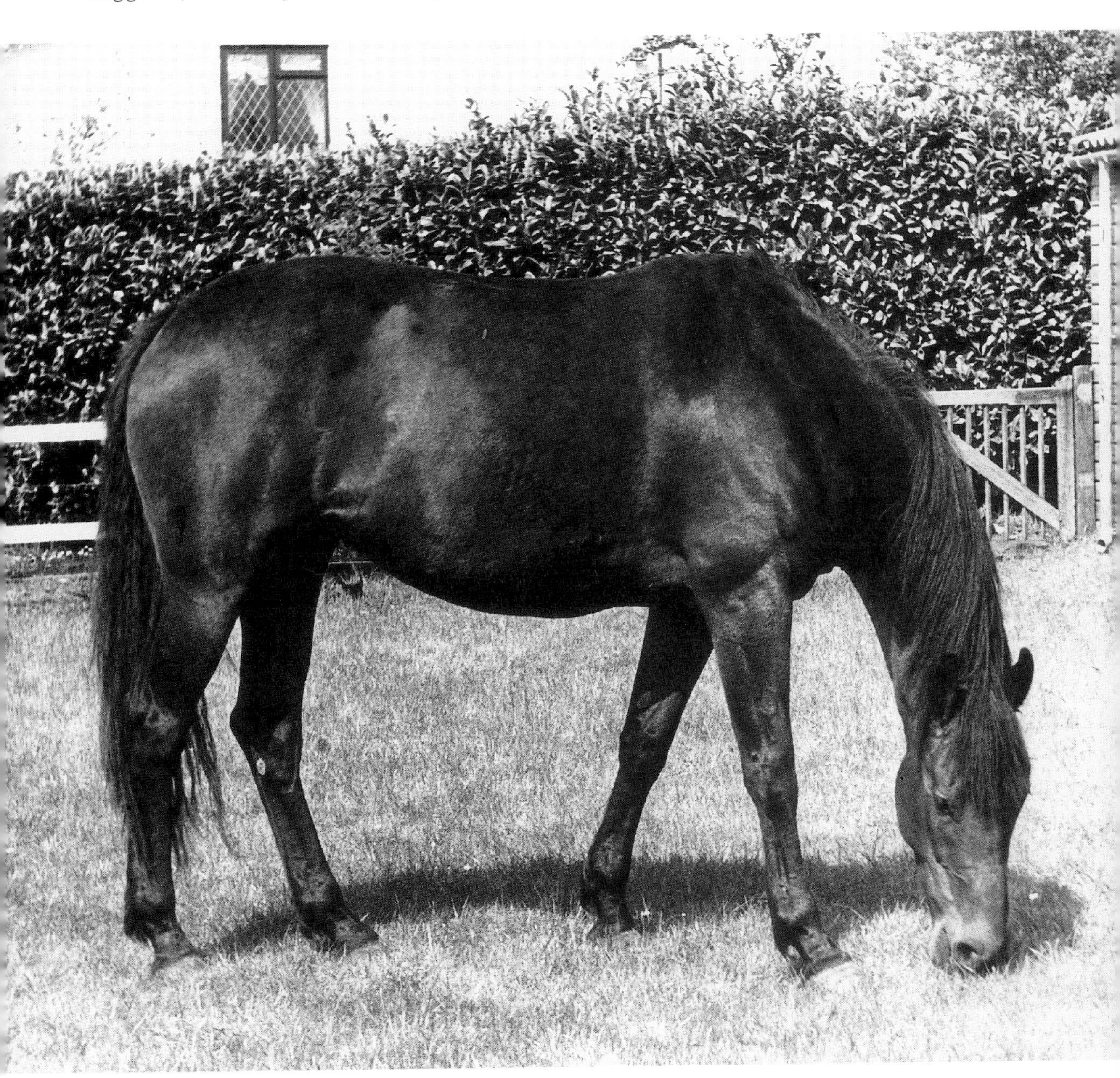

3 Buying a foal before it is weaned is also a possibility

4 Horses are very gregarious creatures, and a youngster especially should not be kept alone after being weaned

would be acceptable, a playmate of his own age is preferable **(4)**.

From the time a horse reaches his first birthday up until his second birthday, he is classed as a yearling (thoroughbred horses are slightly different, in that they are all classed as yearlings from the first of January each year). A horse's first year is a time of playfulness. He will experiment and explore, and, unless he is handled firmly at this age, problems can develop. It is natural, for instance, for a horse to bite and kick. Just watch two yearlings in the field to see this sort of behaviour at its best! This is therefore the time when you will need to teach your yearling to respect the human race.

If you are starting with a horse that is two or three years old, your job should be a little easier, provided that he has been handled correctly. Remember, however, that a youngster which has not been handled correctly can often bring more problems than one which has not been handled at all.

What horse for what purpose?

There are no guidelines as to what breed will be more suited to one area than another, although some breeds are clearly not suited to certain activities **(5)** and **(6)**. There are also, of course, many variations in between. In general, however, rather than the breed of the horse determining his suitability for an activity, it is the *stamp* of the horse which we need to take more as a guide.

Most people who wish to event, for instance, look for a well-put-together thoroughbred or 7/8ths-bred horse with good bone, to ensure speed and stamina and that the horse is up to weight. For dressage, athletic, elastic movement is vital, while good conformation is essential for a show horse. Show jumpers, on the other hand, come in all sorts of shapes and sizes, and those considered most likely to have a good jump often prove otherwise.

This brings us back to the beginning. Whatever the horse's breed or size, you can only bring out his natural abilities, and should not set out to buy a 7/8ths-bred *eventer* or a warmblood *dressage* horse, although it is worth studying the records,

5 It is clear that a shire horse will not make a good eventer

performance and temperament of the sire and dam, as well as noting the successes and failures of closely related stock. Some stallions or lines are noted for their bad temperaments, or vice versa, and much attention should be paid to this when considering a young horse.

In the USA, equestrianism has developed rather differently. Many competitions are much more *breed* orientated, with each breed having its own big events. Breed classes are organized for the Appaloosa, Quarter horse, Tennessee Walker, the Morgan and the American Saddlebred, to name but a few, and require far more of horse and rider than a simple show, as in UK classes. Each horse will be expected to perform in ways characteristic of its breed, performing tasks for which it was originally bred. Someone wishing to compete in such classes will obviously try to breed or acquire a horse which is an excellent example of its breed.

6 Nor is a pure-bred Arab likely to make a good show jumper

Assessing suitability

While you cannot select an untrained horse secure in the knowledge that he *will* perform well in your chosen sphere, you can cut down on the likelihood of choosing a horse which will turn out to be totally unsuitable.

His character will play perhaps the most important part in your success, and is something that you should consider carefully before training of any sort commences. While the horse is still untrained, you can gauge his temperament and character by the way that he acts towards you and towards other horses.

GOOD ATTRIBUTES TO LOOK FOR IN THE YOUNGSTER

- **Calmness**: the young horse should not over-react to unknown situations. He may want to look at new objects or take stock of a new situation before complying with our wishes, but he should not take one look and bolt, with no regard for his handler.
- **A good temperament**: this is obviously important, as no one training their own horse wants to have to deal with a horse which constantly tries to bite or kick them.
- **Willingness**: while a horse may be calm and generally good-tempered, it does not automatically follow that he will be a willing participant in all that we ask of him. Horses have a very limited reasoning power, so it is essential to have a horse who is willing to listen and to try.
- **Trust**: horses are generally very trusting creatures, and we should preserve this at all costs. It is because of such trust that we are able to accomplish so much with them. We must be able to distinguish between naughtiness, nervousness and misunderstanding, and our actions towards each type of behaviour should be clear and consistent.
- **Character**: a horse's character will largely be determined by all the preceding factors. However, a calm, good-tempered, willing and trusting horse is still capable of having a bit of sparkle – and this should not be repressed. It is with just such a horse that we will be able to form the happy partnership so essential to successful training.

Previous history

The more that you know about a horse's past, the better. Many people feel they will be able to re-train a spoilt horse, and the reduction in price of such an animal may often seem attractive. Training horses is not an easy task, however, and finding solutions to the added problems that a bad history can bring is often only within reach of the most experienced of trainers.

A horse learns by repetition. We cannot hope to plant a seed and watch it grow, as the horse's mind simply does not work in such a way. Rather, we look to the horse's memory to help us to train him, and, because he has such a good memory, we must be careful in all our actions towards him. The horse will associate new situations with past experiences, and mistakes at a young age can therefore be very detrimental to future training.

Take the yearling which is being loaded into a trailer for a show. Breeder A has taken two weeks before the show to get the youngster used to the trailer. She has allowed him to sniff it, to walk up the ramp at his own pace, and to take several days before he was confident enough to walk into the trailer, when he was instantly rewarded with a feed. He was then allowed to feed in the trailer each day, until it was second nature for him to walk into the trailer and stand quietly. He was then taken on short trips, until, four days later, he was expected to load.

Breeder B had decided not to attempt to box her yearling until the morning of the show, as she knew that he was an amenable horse and would offer little resistance.

On the morning of the show, both horses were prepared for travelling with boots, rugs and tail bandages. Breeder A's horse sensed that something was different and hesitated at the bottom of the ramp, but after a pause remembered his earlier lessons and, trusting his breeder, bounded up the ramp to await his reward.

Breeder B's horse appeared to be calm, and, after a look into the dark box, cautiously stepped on to the ramp, only to jump straight off again when the hollow noise of the ramp planks frightened him, unfortunately landing straight on his breeder's foot. Breeder B asked her groom to swish a lungeing whip behind her yearling. The horse became so terrified that he jumped up the ramp, and, smiling, breeder B slammed it shut.

Yearling A arrived at the show a little nervous but was soon calmed by his owner. He was shown in his class, and then taken home.

Yearling B arrived at the show dripping with sweat, was terribly tucked up and could not attend his class after all. Breeder B was furious, and, when the yearling decided not to go anywhere near the box once he was unloaded, she proceeded to shout at him and smack him. He was eventually boxed for the journey home by four strong men, and, once home, was turned out, never to be shown again.

Yearling A associates boxing with pleasure and reward, and will travel anywhere. Yearling B, having been left in his field, has forgotten all about the experience – that is, until you come to buy him! You like him and hand over your money, and breeder B kindly offers to deliver him. Along with her four strong helpers, she manages to get him boxed up and he arrives at your yard, dripping with sweat and very nervous, which, after all 'is only natural for a youngster changing homes', as breeder B tells you.

Yearling B has had two bad experiences

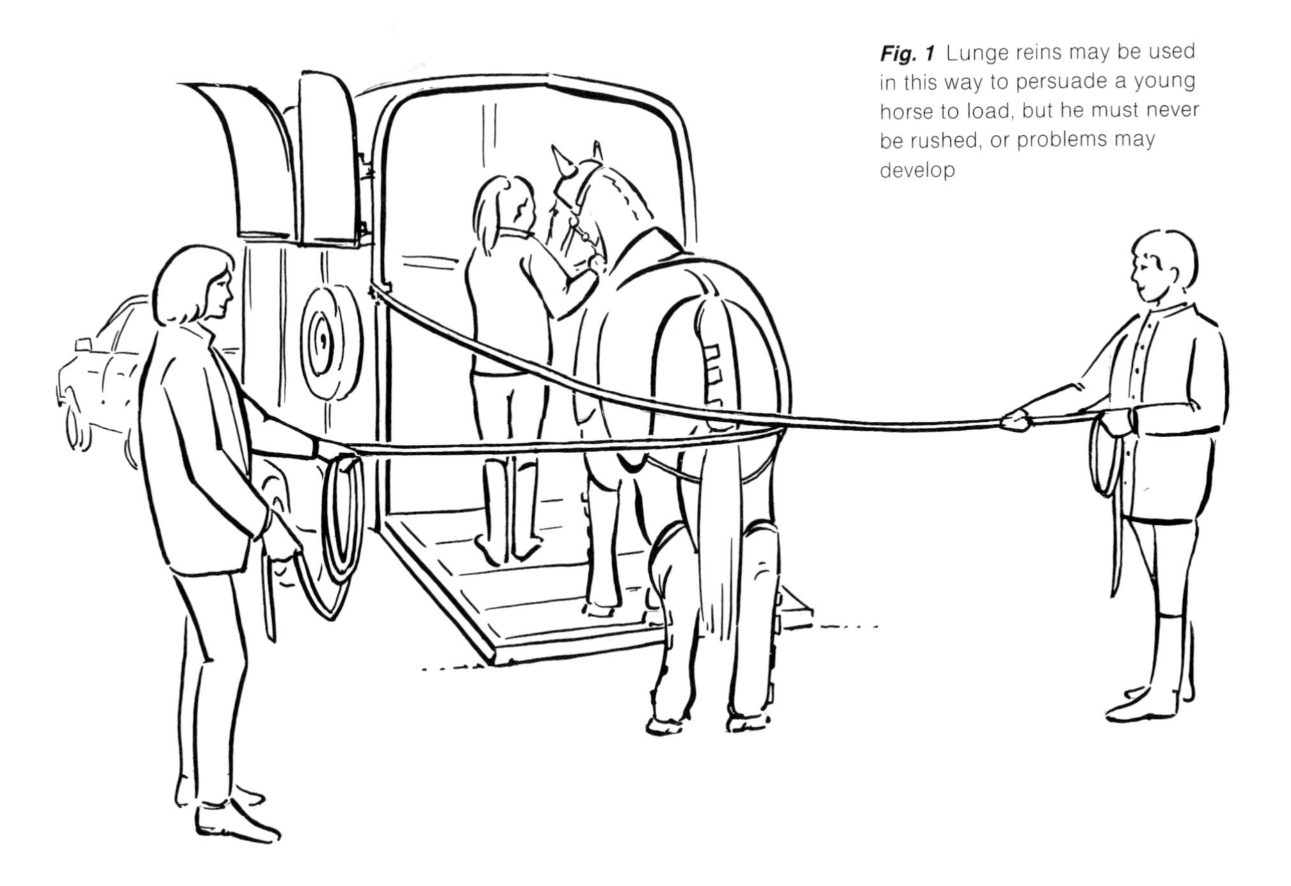

Fig. 1 Lunge reins may be used in this way to persuade a young horse to load, but he must never be rushed, or problems may develop

of boxing which he will never forget; but, as you are unaware of what has gone before, it will fall to you to find this out the next time you come to box him. There are ways of inducing a nervous horse to load without fear **(fig. 1)**, but such methods will require a great deal of patience on your part, and even then the horse treated badly as a youngster is always likely to be an unwilling and nervous traveller.

This story clearly indicates that it is vital to ask searching questions about a youngster's previous history, and to satisfy yourself that he has not set up bad associations to things that you will particularly wish him to do. His handling before you acquire him should have been enjoyable, so that he associates situations that he encounters with pleasure and reward. In this way, his obedience will have been formed by habits which have become second nature to him.

If, on the other hand, his handling has been upsetting, he will associate new situations that he encounters with apprehension, and, more probably, with fright or even pain. He will therefore become obstinate, and, because his new owner does not understand him, his trust will diminish even more and a vicious circle will emerge. In this situation, without sympathy and understanding, the horse will simply get worse.

Conformation

Good conformation cannot be created in a horse, so it is important to recognize a well-made horse from the outset **(7)**. You should be able to distinguish between a

7 Good conformation should be a primary consideration when choosing a youngster

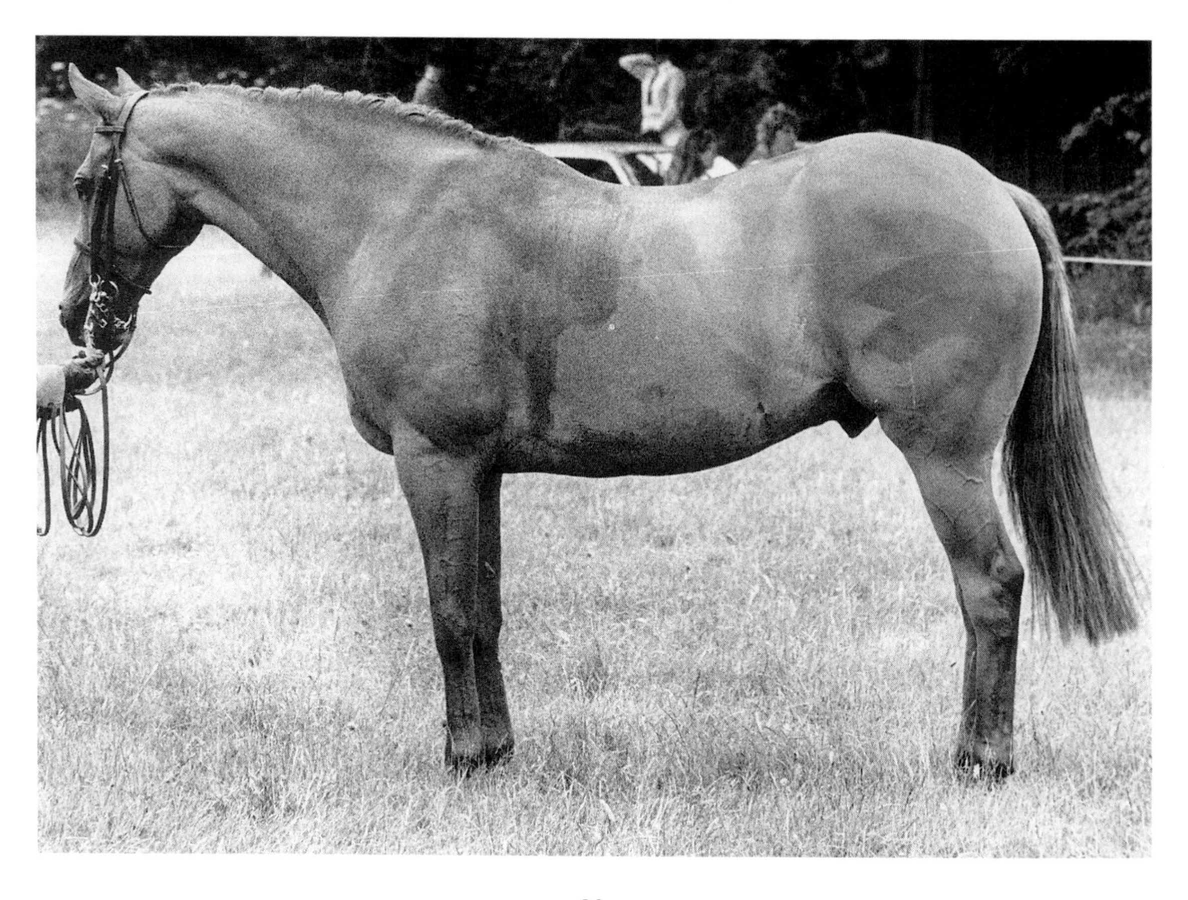

horse which may be in poor condition, yet still has good conformation, and one which is very well conditioned but lacks good conformation.

Certain 'tricks of the trade' can disguise a horse's bad points, but they will always be evident to someone who knows what they are looking for. Faults in conformation may often be a pointer to certain weaknesses, and are a warning that the horse may not stand up to the rigours of training for a particular competitive sphere **(8)**.

No two horses are the same, but, nevertheless, there are certain desirable characteristics for which to look in any potential riding or competition horse **(9)**.

8 A youngster with very poor conformation is more likely to suffer from lameness or other problems in later life, and will not provide a smooth, balanced ride

The neck

This should be straight or slightly arched, and in proportion in length to rest of the body. It should not be too thick-set, nor too weak. The neck should come out of the shoulder at the correct angle, without over-development of the lower muscles.

The head

The head should be intelligent, with a broad forehead and large, kind eyes. It should also be in proportion to the rest of the body, with large, well-defined nostrils. The lower teeth should meet the upper teeth; if they are behind the upper teeth the horse is described as 'parrot-mouthed', a condition which may impair his ability to graze properly. The head must be well-set on to the neck, with plenty of breathing

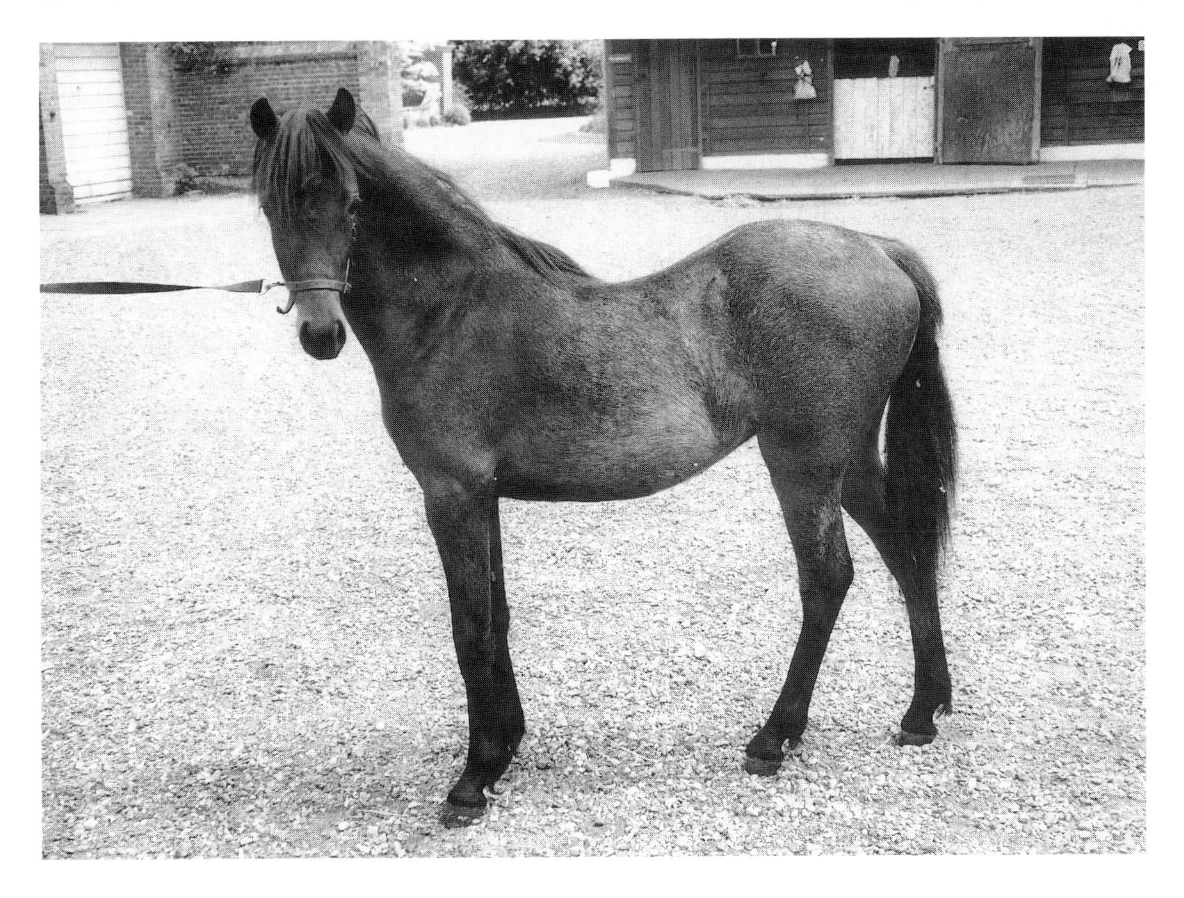

9 Quality is always apparent, whether the horse is in show condition or out at grass, as this two-year-old demonstrates

space between the lower jaw bones near the throat.

The shoulder

These should be long and sloping from the withers to the point of the shoulder. A horse with this conformation will be a more comfortable ride, as a short, upright shoulder produces a shorter stride.

The withers

The withers should be prominent (but not too cresty), gently tapering away into the back.

The back

This should be short and strong, and neither dipped nor too wide.

The hindquarters

The quarters should be straight, strong and broad, reaching well down into the second thigh.

The chest

The chest should not be too narrow, as this will bring the forelegs closer together.

The girth

This should be deep, and the ribs well-sprung.

The forearms

These should be strong with plenty of muscle.

The knees

The knees need to be broad and flat to take the weight of the body. The forearm bone and the cannon bone should be in a straight line, with an evenly placed knee.

The cannon bones

The cannon bones should be strong and short with clearly defined tendons behind them. The amount of *bone* that a horse has refers to the measurement of the whole lower limb region, just below the knee.

The pasterns

These should be sloping and set at a gentle angle. Upright pasterns prevent the buffering of concussion on the joints, and pasterns which are too sloping allow strain to be taken on the suspensory ligament and tendons.

The hooves

These should be deep, with adequate room between the heels, as narrow, 'boxy' feet can restrict the function of the foot. The frog should be firm and well-developed, with a shallow depression in the centre.

The hind thighs

These should be long, well-muscled and well-let down, with strong second thighs (gaskins). Thoroughbred horses tend to be longer in the thighs and straighter in the hind legs, which enables them to gallop. Dressage horses or show jumpers need to be much stronger through their hind legs with their hocks well under them, in order to enable them to produce collection and spring.

The hocks

The hocks should be large and fairly square, with the point of the hocks well-defined.

There must, of course, be some scope for variation in the above points, as, if we were to find a horse with such conformation, he would be a rare animal indeed. However, a good type of horse should possess most of the above qualities.

Action

A horse with good conformation is also likely to have good action. Paces should be straight, active, elastic and rhythmical, with equal stride lengths. It is desirable to watch a horse loose in the field, as he will show his true paces uninhibited by his handler **(10)**.

When selecting a horse, you should ask for him to be trotted straight towards you and then past you. You should take note of his way of going. Does he move straight? Are his strides free and easy? Does he brush, dish or forge?

It is unlikely that the untrained youngster with good conformation will be unsound, unless he has suffered some kind of injury or disease. You should therefore be wary of any youngster which does not

Fig. 2 It is advisable to have any potential purchase vetted

trot up sound without an obvious reason, such as having been kicked in the field. In any event, it would be advisable to have him vetted, including lower-leg x-rays, as these will show up potential hazards not evident from appearance alone.

Having a horse that you intend to buy vetted will also save you money in the long run, as most insurance firms now insist on the production of a current veterinary certificate before they will insure the animal **(fig. 2)**.

Health and happiness

By taking all aspects of horses' behaviour into consideration we can learn to understand them better as individuals, and therefore motivate each to work happily for us. The horse which does something because he wishes to do so will always try harder than the horse which does something out of pain or fear. We need to be able to recognize our horses' emotions and respond to them correctly in order to gain their respect.

A happy horse is more likely to be a healthy horse, and a healthy horse is one which can be trained well. He is more likely to be receptive to our ideas, whereas the unhappy horse may often be confused, and block his mind to our requests.

It is therefore very important to get to know your horse before you embark upon any form of training. Once you have established a level of communication in this way, your task of trying to convey your wishes will be far easier. Both you and your horse will probably still make mistakes, but, because you can communicate, you will be able to work through them.

10 The loose horse should exhibit athleticism with a natural swing through his body, making for a comfortable ride in the future

The handler's/trainer's role

It is sensible to ask yourself what qualities you have in order to start your horse safely and well. Although you may be able to elicit the help of a willing assistant with the task of starting your horse, the real burden of doing so competently will fall on your shoulders alone.

Try to evaluate your own strengths and weaknesses as a trainer. This will enable you to be prepared for awkward situations should they arise, and perhaps to formulate a plan to avoid them altogether. If, for example, you are not sure how brave you will be when it comes to backing your horse for the first time, try to arrange for someone who has no such qualms to do the job for you. Don't wait and hope for the best – be prepared.

Your own riding ability needs to be sound when it comes to further schooling of the youngster, but this is not to say that you need to be the world's greatest dressage rider. However, you do need to be totally honest with yourself about your own abilities, and whether or not you are up to the task of training a young horse.

Self-evaluation

At the outset, consider carefully your reasons for wanting to train a youngster, rather than letting a professional handle the job. The worst reason for doing so is because of the costs involved. Buying a young, unridden youngster because an older, trained horse is too expensive is foolhardy. Firstly, it would probably cost you just as much to keep and train the horse as it would to buy the older horse, after saving up during the years that you would otherwise have spent in training the youngster. Secondly, it will probably cost much more if you end up having to have the horse sorted out by a professional

– if that is still possible – because you had neither the patience nor the self-discipline needed to carry the training through to a successful completion.

Successful trainers, including 'first timers' are usually those who enjoy the starting process itself, rather than simply regarding it as a means to producing the riding horse that they want.

The trainer's temperament

Horses are very susceptible to human moods. They can sense your emotions and interpret tense and worried behaviour, which also tends to make them edgy. It is therefore best to start early training sessions only when you are in a calm and confident frame of mind. You should also be alert at all times, and remember that tiredness may affect your reactions: if your horse gets the better of you through inattention, you will have given him endless scope to try to misbehave another time. Try to start any sessions with a clear mind which is focused on the job in hand.

WHAT MAKES A GOOD TRAINER?

To ensure that you are temperamentally suited to the task of training youngsters, you should consider the following.

- Do you have the patience to adjust the training routine to your horse's physical and mental capabilities as necessary?
- Do you have the required confidence and courage?
- Do you have the tact to be able to choose the appropriate course of action by recognizing the horse's state of mind?
- Do you have the self-discipline to resist the temptation of asking too much too soon because of your own drive to succeed?
- Would you be able to keep calm in any situation, thinking things through rationally?
- Sacrifices are likely to be needed before you have finished the training, so are you totally dedicated?

The voice

The trainer's voice plays a very important role in educating the young horse successfully. Used quietly and soothingly, it encourages the horse and promotes confidence. A raised tone (as opposed to shouting, which serves little purpose), on the other hand, conveys to the horse that some sort of correction is needed in his behaviour.

The voice is the one thing throughout the training period which remains constant. Your horse will have become accustomed to your voice throughout his early handling, and will have learned the meaning of certain words by the tone that you use when giving verbal instructions. This is extremely useful when it comes to lungeing and long reining. A few basic words completely understood by the horse will enable you to manoeuvre him without confusion.

Key words are: *walk-on*, which is said in a light, brisk tone; *teerrot*, which is said in a slightly higher tone to encourage the horse to trot on; *canter-up*, which is said in a light, brisk tone, slightly higher than when asking the horse to trot on; *whooa*, in a low, soothing tone to let the horse know to slow down into trot or walk as desired; and, finally, *stanD*, with an emphasized 'D'. The horse also learns very quickly to respond to *good boy/girl* by relaxing, and to *no* by paying more attention.

It is a good idea to call your horse frequently by name, as this will let him know that you are talking to him when he is in the presence of other horses. Other such words are *over boy/girl*, when asking the horse to move away from you in the stable, and *give it up* when asking him to lift his feet.

With these few key words understood, you will have a horse which is good-mannered in the stable, will walk on and stand when in-hand, and will respond to instructions when beginning his training.

Actions

The horse responds less well to actions, especially if they are given without a verbal command (except, of course, in the case of the ridden horse, where he learns to respond to his rider's aids).

Any actions which are given, however, such as laying a hand on the horse in the stable to encourage him to move over, should be light and clear. A great slap is not necessary. Contrary to popular belief, the horse does not like to be patted strongly. If you teach the horse to respond to light handling from the beginning, he will never need anything stronger.

Reasoning

Perhaps one of the best qualities of a good trainer is the ability to apply reasonable doubt. If something goes wrong, the good trainer will not be quick to blame the horse, but will look towards his own actions first. Did I try to ask too much? Did I ask clearly enough? Is the horse tired? Am I tired? The good trainer will always give the benefit of the doubt to the horse initially. If he subsequently becomes satisfied that his actions were correct, he will then ask the horse to respond again before taking any disciplinary action.

It never pays to pick an argument with a horse unnecessarily. When teaching the youngster to lead in-hand, for instance, why ask him to lead away from his companions, when he will happily obey you if you ask him to lead towards them? Once he is familiar with leading, he can then be expected to obey you further by walking away when asked.

One final but important point to remember is that you should always be certain the horse is capable of doing what you ask, both physically and mentally.

KEY POINTS

- Starting with an unspoilt horse which is sound in mind and body is of paramount importance, especially to someone attempting to train their own horse for the first time.
- Whether to buy or breed is a matter of choice depending on your personal circumstances, but bear in mind that neither method is a guarantee of ending up with an animal which suits you.
- Rather than the breed of the horse determining his suitability for an activity, it is the *stamp* of a horse which you should take as more of a guide, coupled with good conformation and temperament.
- Whatever the horse's breed or size, you can only bring out his natural abilities.
- Obedience is developed through habit, by the association of ideas, so you should aim to make the habit of obedience second nature to the horse.
- The horse has a good memory, and we must therefore be careful in all our actions towards him.
- Good behaviour should be quickly and consistently rewarded, so that the horse associates obedience with pleasure.
- As a trainer, you must be able to distinguish between fright, naughtiness and misunderstanding.
- The qualities of a good trainer are: self-control, confidence, patience, sympathy, skill, determination and tact.
- The voice is an extremely important aid in educating youngsters.

2

EARLY EDUCATION

A word about punishment and reward

The most successful way of dealing with youngsters of any age is to adopt a system of punishment and reward. They soon learn that reward follows correct behaviour, and that punishment follows undesirable behaviour.

It must be clear what you mean by punishment. If the horse has not behaved in the required manner, you may decide that – after you have considered your own actions – the horse needs to be corrected, or he will not learn what is required. Never lose your temper and hit the horse, or shout at him, as this will only confuse him, but correct him by withholding the expected reward, whether it be 'good boy/girl', or a friendly pat.

If further correction is needed, the lesson should be repeated and the tone of the voice strengthened, but words and instructions should still be familiar. You must always make sure that the horse knows what he is being punished for. In this way, the horse will not become frightened or nervous when he does something wrong, but will seek to do as you ask in search of reward.

The misuse of punishment in early training is one of the worst errors that can be made. By punishing wrongly, a friendly, willing and confident animal can be reduced to a permanently timid, anxious and distrustful horse.

The foal

The education of any horse should begin when he is still a foal. Some breeders prefer not to do much with their foals until they are weaned, but this is often a case of convenience and can make the weanling much more difficult to handle later on.

There is much that can be done with a foal, and a correct start at this age can make all the difference between a horse totally trusting the human race or not. A foal can be touched from the minute it is born, although this is often difficult if the mare is foal-proud **(11)**.

Accepting the foaling slip

The first thing that a foal should learn to accept is a foaling slip **(fig. 3)**. This will enable him to be led, which is preferable to leaving him to follow his dam. In preparation for fitting the foaling slip, you should accustom your foal to being touched. Run your hands all over his body and caress behind his ears, talking to him all the time so that he becomes used to

11 Even the quietest of mares can become very protective of her foal, and in such cases it is sensible to give them some time alone before you attempt to handle the foal

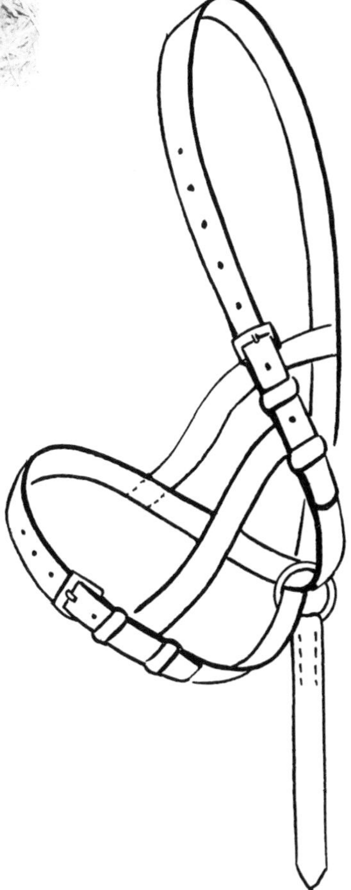

Fig. 3 The foaling slip enables the foal to be led from an early age

your voice. A very young foal can twist and damage his neck from a slip, and therefore could first be led with a stable rubber round his neck before the slip is introduced. This method can be useful for a weak foal, although may be less successful if the foal is strong.

The easiest way to introduce the foaling slip is to stand at the foal's near-side shoulder, facing forwards, and to back him gently into a corner of the stable. Holding the slip in your left hand, place your right hand over the foal's neck, grasp the slip in both hands, and gently but quickly ease it on to his muzzle and do it up **(fig. 4)**. This lesson can be repeated every day, and the slip left on for longer periods, until the foal shows no concern. He should also accept you holding him from the slip, and should not be allowed to pull away from you.

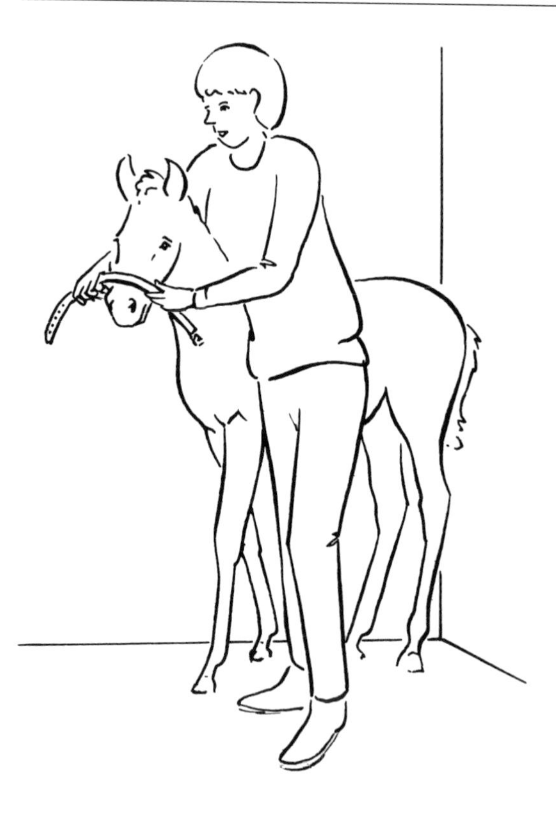

Fig. 4 Introducing the foaling slip

Simple lessons

Once the foal is used to human contact, simple lessons can begin. He can be taught to pick up his feet in turn, and, as he will not be very strong, this should cause few problems. He will then easily accept the farrier rasping his feet at regular intervals when the mare is shod **(fig. 5)**. The foal can also be groomed with a soft brush, while someone else holds him. He should never be tied up at this age.

Learning to lead is another lesson which can be taught. When starting to lead a foal, two people are needed – one for the mare, the other for the foal. Lead the foal alongside or behind the mare, and gently encourage him forward by putting an arm around his quarters and gently pushing, while keeping a tight hold on the foaling slip **(12)**.

In the next few months, the foal should learn to lead from either side of the mare, and to accept being led in front or further behind her. There is no better teacher than a foal's dam, and he will soon begin to copy her actions. This can be extremely valuable when it comes to catching him. Whenever you try to catch a foal, you should always reward him when he comes

12 Encourage the foal to follow his dam by gently pushing him foreward in this way

straight away. He will then gain confidence in his association with you, and will eagerly await your call.

Showing the foal along with his dam will also be of great benefit **(13)**. He will come to accept things such as boxing, travelling, being led in-hand, noise and crowds, all of which would otherwise have to be learned at a later stage when he is both bigger and stronger.

It is a mistake to coddle a foal, as this only encourages bolshy behaviour, and a balance must be maintained between kindness and firmness. He must be corrected if he behaves badly, and rewarded if he behaves well.

The weanling

Before the foal is weaned, at about six months, he should have been introduced to hard feed. He should not be weaned until he is eating well. Some breeders wean their foals by totally separating them from their dams on a given day, but this can be traumatic. For the owner who

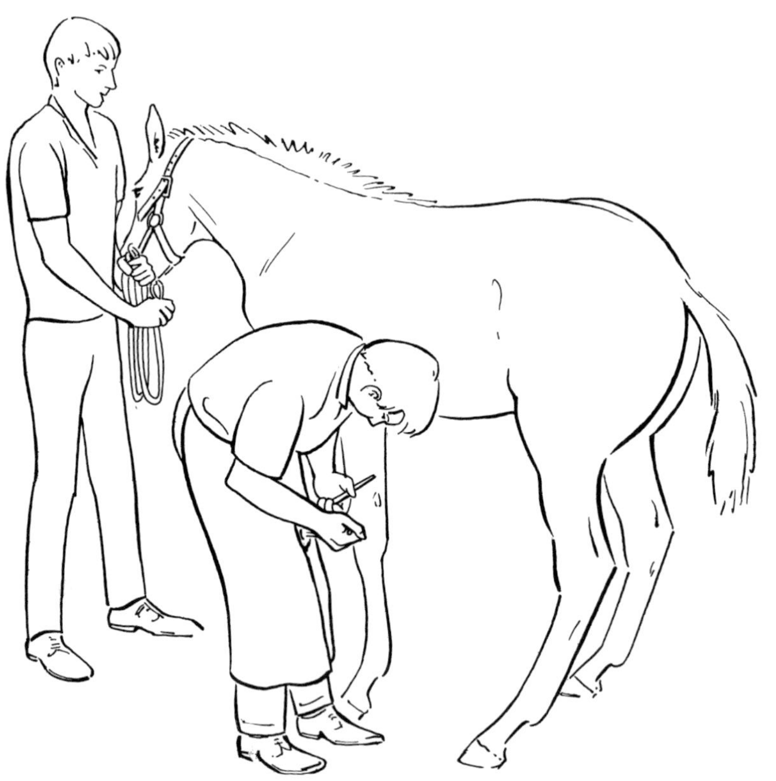

Fig. 5 You should accustom the foal to having his feet picked up so that he will stand quietly to have his feet rasped by the farrier, which should be done at regular intervals

13 Showing a foal along with his dam will familiarize him with unusual sights and sounds, and teach him to stand quietly

has just one mare and foal, weaning can be introduced more gradually.

The mare can be taken away for periods at a time, with the foal being left with a suitable companion (another foal, or foals, if possible), until, in the end, the dam is removed altogether **(14)**.

14 If possible, foals should be weaned together to provide company for each other

Tying up

There are many things which can be taught during the weanling's first winter, including being tied up without resistance. To achieve this successfully, put on him a headcollar or halter which fits snugly. This should be attached to a strong rope and tied with a quick-release knot to a secure tethering ring, preferably one in a wall **(15)** and **(16)**. If the weanling

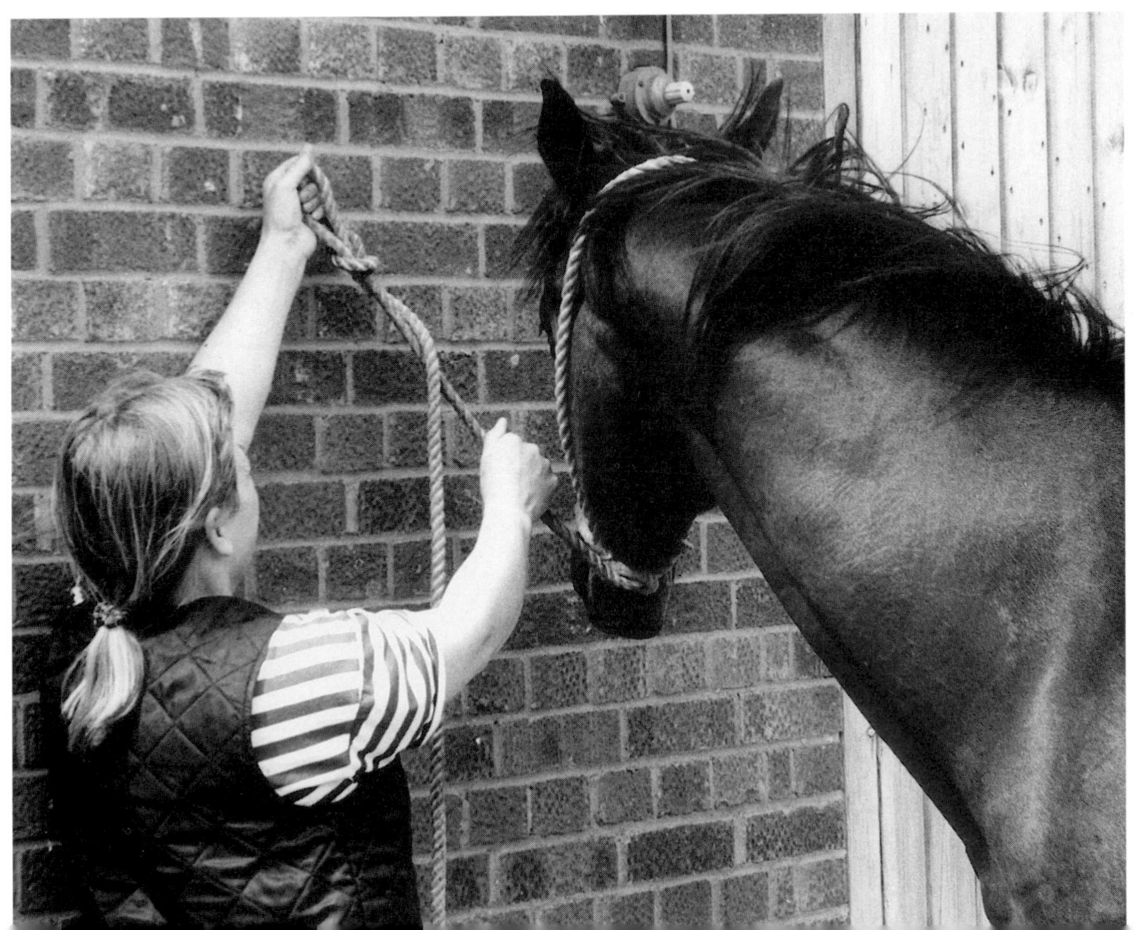

15 Tying up: the youngster should be tied using a quick-release knot

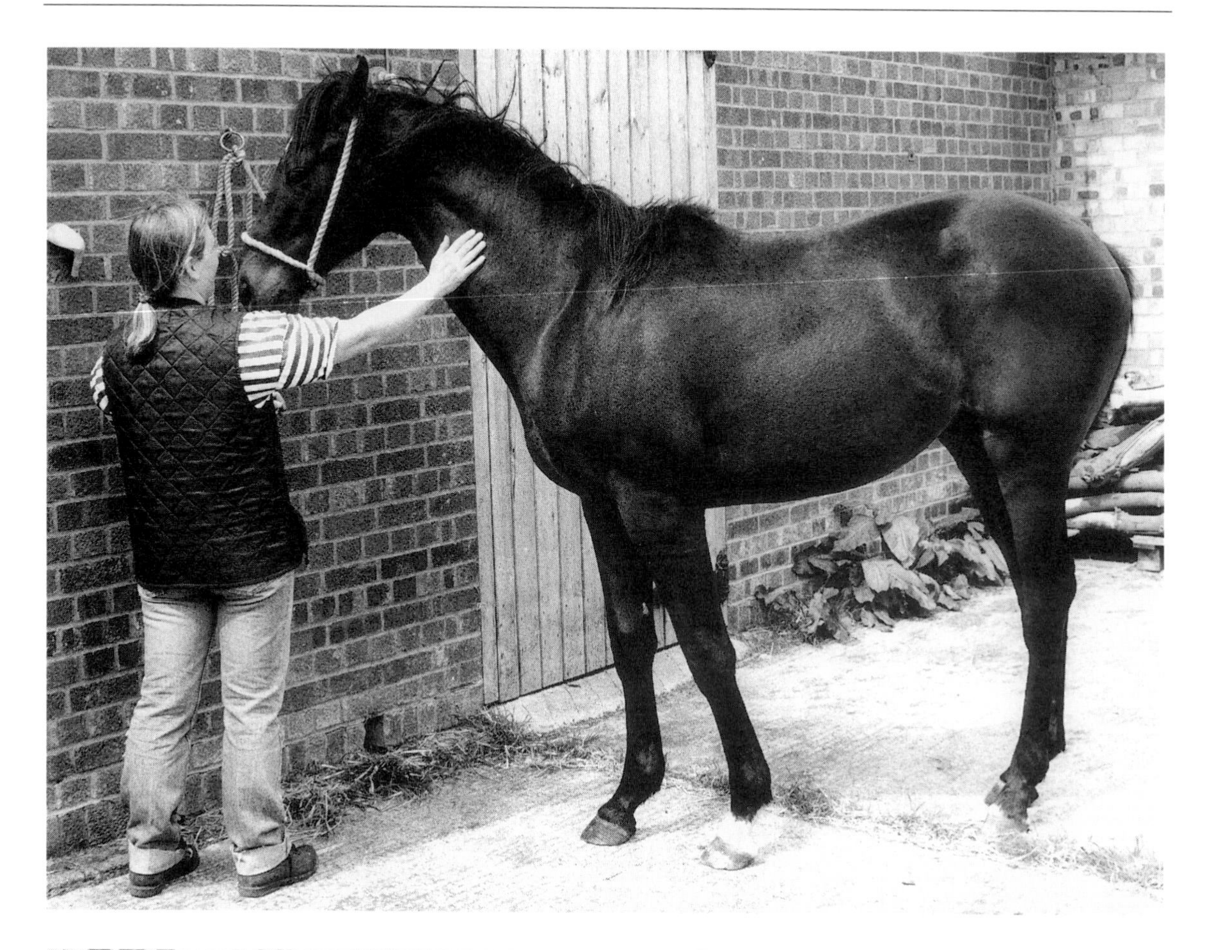

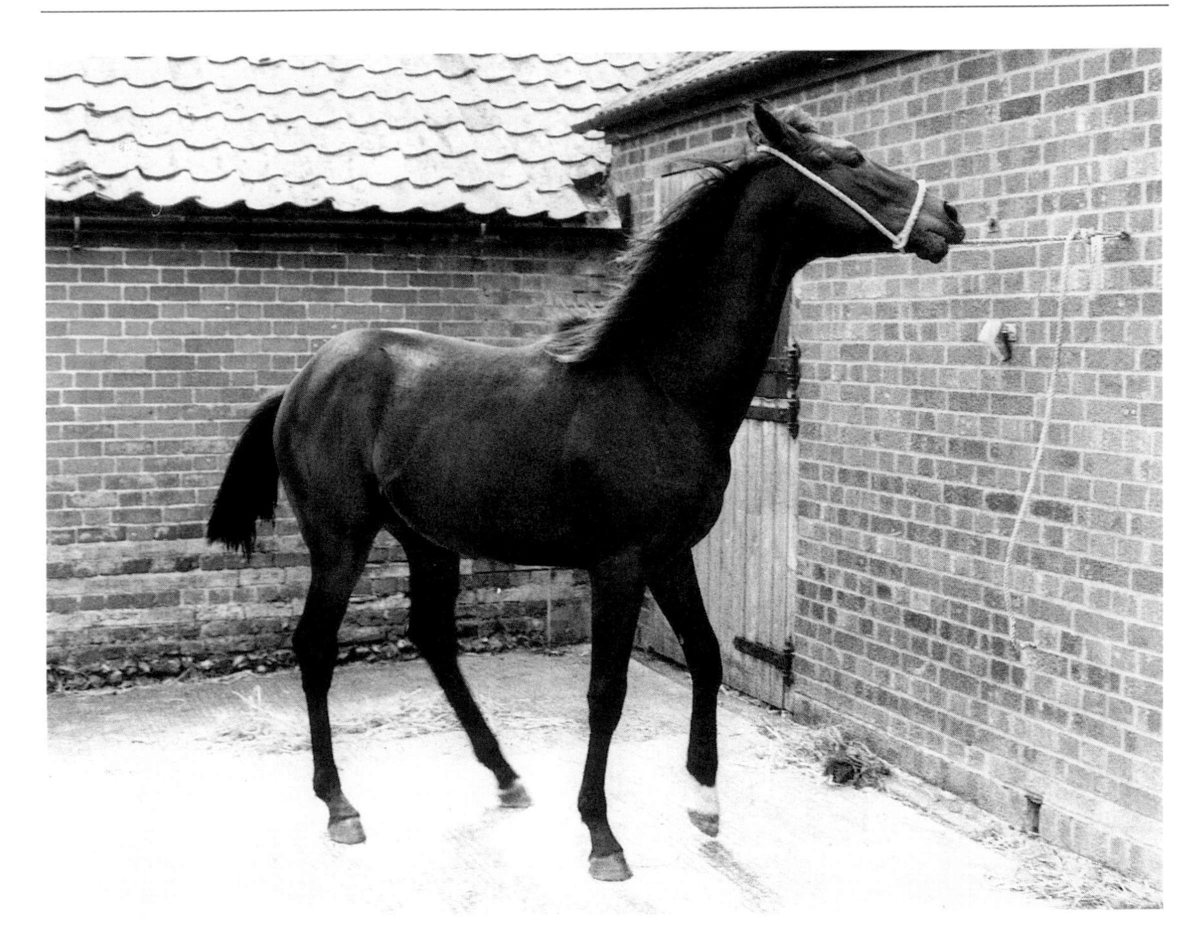

16 *(Top left)* He is then stroked to reassure him before the trainer stands back to observe his reaction once he realizes that he is tied up (*note:* he should NEVER be left unattended)

17 *(Bottom left)* If the horse attempts to pull back, it is vital that nothing snaps. He will soon realize that it is useless to try to free himself (*note:* the end of the rope could easily be pulled to free the horse in an emergency)

18 *(Above)* As a result, he soon begins to accept the situation and concedes (*note:* he is tied in a safe area without any implements or objects that he could knock over or become entangled in)

attempts to pull back, he will realize that it is useless to try to free himself, and will soon accept being tied without pulling back **(17)** and **(18)**.

The weanling should not be left tied up without supervision at any time, as he will not be able to release himself in an emergency. Once he has learned the lesson of tying up, it is safer to tie the rope on to a piece of bailing twine, attached to the ring, which will break in an emergency **(19)**.

Stable manners

This is also the time for the youngster to learn a few stable manners. Even if he is not stabled, he will benefit from being brought in each day and fed in the stable.

You should teach him to 'move over' at your command, reinforcing your verbal instruction by gently pushing him over with your hand. The horse must learn to keep out of your way when required, to enable you to take care of his needs such as mucking out and watering while he is still in the stable.

Think about where you wish the horse

to move, and make it clear to him where you want him to be. If you want him to move backward, away from you, stand in front of him and slightly to the side before giving your command. If you want him to move forward, away from you, stand at his hip (behind his eye) before giving the command. By strategically positioning yourself in this way, you can make it very clear to the horse what you require.

The youngster should also respect you whenever you enter the stable, especially when you are carrying his feed. He should be made to 'wait' until you have put his feed in the manger and have retreated, before he comes forward. Give the command 'wait' in a strong tone, and, if necessary, hold your hand up flat in front of you to indicate that you require him to back off. This lesson is also useful when you are leading the horse from the stable, as he will learn not to barge through the door when you tell him to 'wait'.

This first winter is also a good time to introduce the weanling to being rugged up. This is normally done only for training purposes, however (see pages 56–60), as, unless he is to be shown early the next year as a yearling, he will benefit more from being roughed off.

If someone is available to help you, ask them to hold the youngster so that you can concentrate on actually rugging him. If you do not have an assistant, you will have to hold the lead rope and proceed with caution. Never tie the youngster up when first introducing something new, as a lot of damage may be done if he becomes startled and tries to free himself.

19 Once the lesson of tying up has been learned, the rope should be tied to a piece of bailing twine attached to the ring in the wall for safety

WORMING AND VACCINATION

- Worming is an essential requirement at this age. Neglecting the worming of a foal or yearling can cause very serious damage through red worm – often many years later.
- Foals and youngstock need to be wormed more often than adult horses, and a wormer which is active against the large white worm needs to be used.
- Your vet will advise on a suitable wormer and worming programme for your situation, and also on a routine programme of vaccination against equine influenza and tetanus, which will start around this time.
- In the United States an eastern and western encephalomyelitis vaccination must also be given. Rhinopheumonitis, rabies and Potomac horse fever are often suggested depending on the region.

The yearling

In his first year of life, the horse will have learned the basic lessons which will enable him to be handled without problems. He does not, therefore, need to be taught much as a yearling, as he will remember his earlier lessons. Many flat racehorses will be lunged and started in the autumn, ready for racing as two-year-olds, but their starting process is designed purely with racing in mind, and so is not one that we will consider in this book. Your aim is to produce a competition or riding horse which is capable both mentally and physically of coping with the demands that our training will put on him. You should therefore not consider starting him at this age, as he will still be growing and maturing.

The yearling can be led about the yard or farm to accustom him to objects which may seem frightening to him **(20)**. Leading him on quiet lanes will also benefit his education towards behaving in traffic **(21)** and **(22)**. This is also a time when he can be taught to load into a trailer or lorry. Getting the young horse used to such activities at this age will be of benefit when it comes to future training, and, by introducing things slowly throughout the year, you will help him to develop confidence and a sound mind. Short, regular sessions will show the most improvement, as the horse will come to accept such activities as second nature. Showing the yearling will also be beneficial to his early education **(23)**.

THE IMPORTANCE OF ROUTINES

- A daily routine should be established early on, as the horse is a creature of habit. He may not be able to tell the time, but he always knows when his breakfast is due. The horse has been domesticated by humans, and the least we can do is to ensure that he feels secure in the environment that we have made for him.
- A known routine provides stability in the horse's life, which in turn ensures his happiness. If you intend to ask the horse to conform to your wishes, you must at all costs preserve this happiness, so you must start as you intend to carry on, and always put the horse before yourself. The rewards will be worth it.

20 Lead the youngster around the yard or farm to familiarize him with unusual objects or vehicles, such as this dumper truck. You should encourage him to walk up to the vehicle and to have a good look

21 *(Top right)* On quiet lanes, walk the youngster back and forth past any vehicles that you meet

22 *(Bottom right)* He will soon learn to accept them without fear

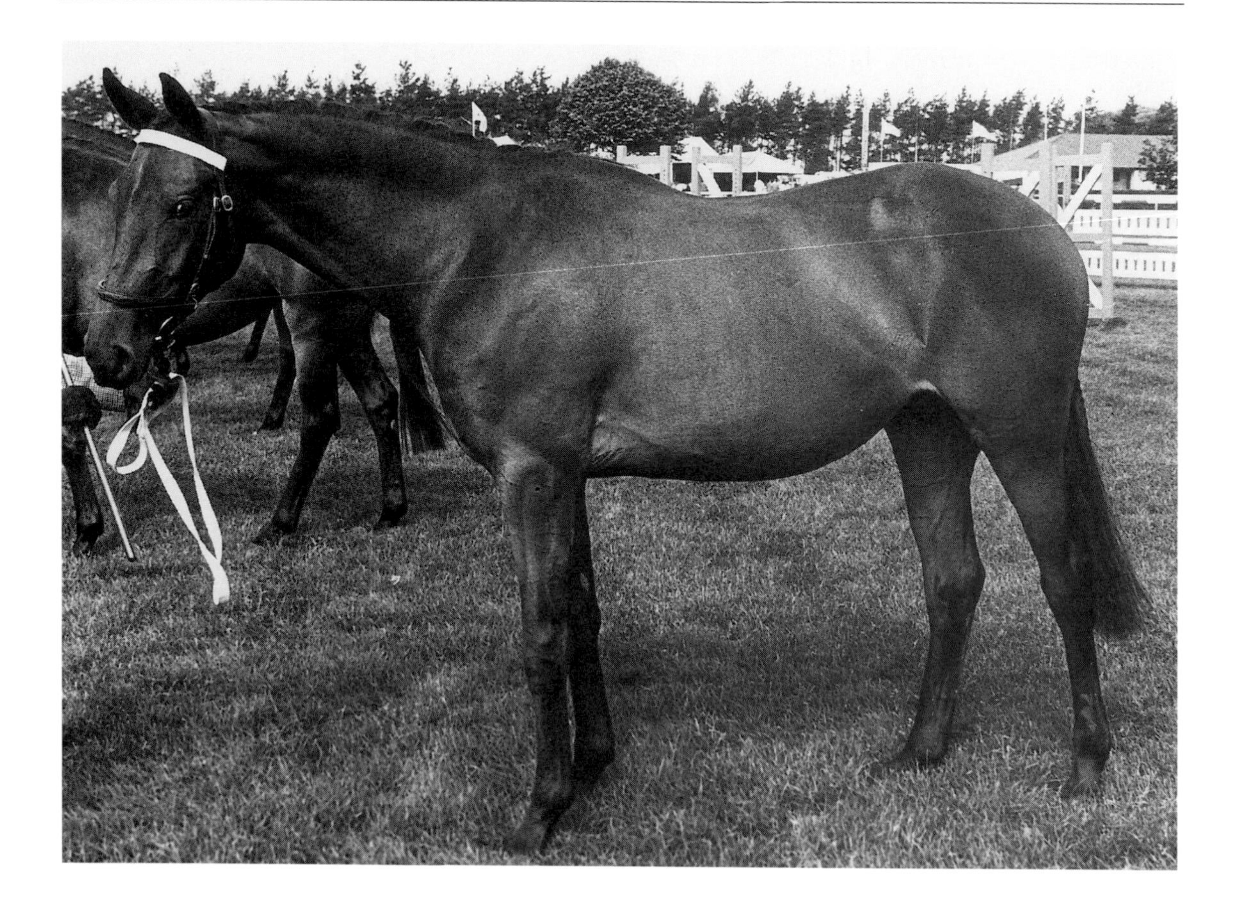

23 Showing the yearling will reinforce his earlier lessons of leading and standing up correctly and patiently

The two-year-old

Once again, previous lessons should be repeated in the spring of the horse's second year, to ensure that he knows how to behave before you attempt to teach him anything new. Although many people teach two-year-olds to lunge, I personally do not recommend this, as moving in circles puts quite a strain on young bones and tendons. The two-year-old will also still be growing, so, in order to be sure that he is mature enough to be started successfully, it is much safer for someone training their own horse for the first time to wait until his third year.

Your patience will pay off, as horses which are started as two-year-olds do not seem to be very far ahead of those started in their third year. The three-year-old will pick up ideas more quickly, and so training will advance more swiftly and surely. You can also ask questions of a three-year-old that you would not ask a two-year-old. You can therefore ask with confidence, and repeat your requests without the fear of him not being able to cope through immaturity.

The three-year-old

In the horse's third year, you can begin his training in earnest (see Chapters 5–7). Lessons should be taken slowly, and one step at a time. A lesson should always be introduced and understood by the horse, before you go on to anything new.

What to feed and why

Feed times are the most important part of the horse's routine, and these should be as regular as possible once the routine has been established. The horse is totally in your control concerning what he eats, and you must therefore provide him with a suitably balanced diet that is relevant to each stage of his growth.

The foal

The foal will be provided with nearly all the necessary nourishment from his mother's milk, and, once he is a little older, will find most of what he needs in good grazing. However, nutrients in the mother's milk decline as lactation continues, and, if the foal does not have access to excellent pasture, he will need creep feeding. The term 'creep' describes an enclosure of which the foal, but not the mare, can gain access to the feed that is put down. There are now specially designed creep feeders on the market, and creep feeding can begin from about three weeks onward.

You must take care neither to over- nor under-feed the foal, so you should keep him away from the mother's ration. Over-eating can lead to rapid growth, which enhances the possibility of the foal developing metabolic bone disease.

The easiest way to ensure that your foal eats all he needs is to use a proprietary brand of properly formulated feed, which is designed to be fed alongside the mare's milk and grass. In this way, you can be sure that he is obtaining the correct supply of minerals, vitamins and protein, along with adequate calcium, phosphorous and trace minerals needed for good bone growth.

A foal should be consuming 0.5 kg (1 lb) of food a day for each month of his life. For example, at three months of age, he will be eating 1.5 kg (3 lb) of food.

The weanling

This is the time when the youngster does most of his growing. He will attain about 80 per cent of his full adult height during this period and should be fed accordingly, but he must also be allowed plenty of exercise.

As the youngster matures, his protein and energy requirements decrease, although he must still receive adequate levels of each if he is to mature correctly. As he grows, his roughage can be increased and his concentrates slightly reduced.

Throughout, the best policy is to stick to one really good brand of rearing diet, and to follow qualified advice, as research continually throws up new evidence and ideas change rapidly. Feed formulations change accordingly, so your youngster will still receive a balanced ration.

There really is no excuse for the non-expert owner to 'add a little bit of this and a little bit of that' because they have heard that it is the new wonder supplement. This only serves to unbalance the otherwise nutritionally balanced mixture.

Foals and weanlings should not be given hay in nets, as they can easily get their feet tangled in the net when playing or jumping about. Hay should preferably be fed on the floor, or from a hayrack if this is not possible.

The yearling

The best thing that you can do with a yearling is to turn him out on to good grazing for his first spring. The aim at this stage is to promote a slow and steady growth, which is achieved through the winter by feeding 40 to 60 per cent roughage with smaller quantities of concentrates.

The rule here is *do not over-feed*. Time must be given to allow the yearling's frame to grow and mature, without the restriction of too much fat. Many more developmental problems emerge due to over-feeding than to under-feeding at this stage. As always, however, each horse must be treated individually. If your youngster seems to be a particularly 'good doer', for instance, and puts on weight rapidly, then you will need to modify his diet by replacing some of the concentrates with quality forage.

The older youngster

Once your horse has a good start, his feeding will need to be considered in the light of his size, body weight and breed. It is obvious that a 16 h.h. thoroughbred will need to be assessed differently from a 15 h.h. cob.

Each horse should be supplied with good-quality hay through the winter, with a balanced supply of concentrates according to his body weight.

To stable or not?

Your decision as to whether or not to stable your youngster over the winter will depend largely on the facilities that are available. If you have a paddock with a good shelter, safe fencing and watering facilities, and other horses with which to turn out the youngster, he will benefit from being given his freedom out in the field, although he should still be brought in to be fed and handled each day **(fig. 6)**. If the weather turns particularly nasty, he should be rugged up for protection if he is a fine breed. Youngsters kept in this way are far less likely to develop dust allergies and/or stable vices **(24)**.

If you do not have these facilities, your youngster will obviously need to be stabled. His stable must be well-ventilated **(fig. 7)**, and he should be turned out to exercise as much as possible. To prevent a dust allergy from beginning, manage him in a dust-free environment and feed him from a rubber tub on the floor **(25)**.

24 *(Right)* Youngsters which are kept in conditions as near as possible to their natural environment are less likely to develop habits such as crib-biting

Fig. 6 *(Below)* The youngster will benefit from being wintered out, as long as a paddock with safe fencing, watering facilities and a good shelter is available

Fig. 7 A properly protected and vented window should be placed in the back of the youngster's stable

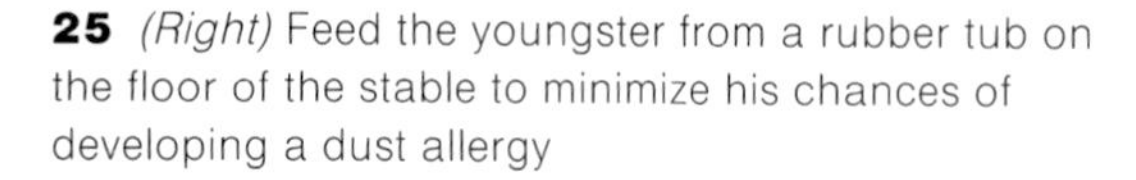

25 *(Right)* Feed the youngster from a rubber tub on the floor of the stable to minimize his chances of developing a dust allergy

Introducing the horse to traffic

The age at which you introduce the horse to traffic will depend on your personal circumstances: whether you have bred or bought your horse, and at what age you acquired him. In either case, I would not recommend that you introduce him to traffic before his first year. If, on the other hand, you have aquired a three-year-old who has never been on the road, it is still not too late to begin.

The very young horse is only acutely aware of what is happening to him at the present time. Taking him out into traffic will completely change his familiar environment, and the hustle and bustle could easily upset him. Although you may feel that a very young horse will be less strong if he decided to misbehave, he will also be less predictable, and you could end up with a loose horse on your hands.

The important issue is how to begin getting him used to traffic, and once you have decided to start, you should formulate a plan. A short walk each day is more beneficial than longer walks, and it is very helpful to have an older horse which is sensible in traffic to lead the way, as the youngster will feel more relaxed and will take his lead from the horse in front.

If you do not know of another horse or pony to go with you, then start by taking your horse on a very quiet lane if possible. Ask any traffic you meet to stop, and be firm in asking your horse to walk past sensibly. Wear a fluorescent tabbard bearing the words *'Slow Please – Young Horse'* to inform motorists from a distance, as safety must be your most important consideration **(fig. 8)**.

Once your horse leads quietly on known lanes, you could take him to a busier road where there is a wide verge, so that you can introduce him to heavier traffic in safety. It is not necessary to insist that the horse walks close to the traffic, as this will scare him unnecessarily. In the absence of a wide verge, you could lead him into a field and allow him to see the traffic in this way. Failing either of these methods, you could box him up and take him to some shows, purely to get him used to some lorries.

Once the horse has shown a responsible attitude towards traffic, he need only be led on the roads occasionally, until ridden work commences.

Fig. 8 A fluorescent tabbard of this type is an important safety precaution with a young horse out on the roads

At what age should a horse be started?

Why is it that most racehorses are on the course as two-year-olds, when horses destined for other spheres are not even backed? The answer to this is a somewhat unfortunate set of circumstances, very different to those in which the owner of the average horse might find himself, and – inevitably, perhaps – in the end it comes down to money.

In the first place, the potential racehorse is both expensive to breed and to buy – the hammer often falls for many thousands of pounds in the sale ring in the hope of acquiring a winner **(26)**. The owner therefore wishes to see a return on his investment as quickly as he can, which puts the trainer under immense pressure to get the horse on to the racecourse as soon as possible. Trainers are, however, only too well aware that many of the horses they train will not even reach the racecourse because their legs will have given way.

The fact that such horses – which have been bred and refined especially with racing in mind – all too often break down is extremely unfortunate, but perhaps more worrying is the trend towards high-performance horses being worked and over-stressed when they are too young.

Why is this worrying? The reason is simple. At a very young age, the horse is neither physically nor mentally mature. Even if he does stand up to training, it is unlikely that he will come through it unscathed, in order to lead a usefully long life as a riding or competition horse. The horse is not a throw-away commodity, yet where are all the seven- and eight-year-old flat racehorses?

The pitfalls of starting a horse too young

The youngster which has been started too young is far more likely to develop stress injuries – lumps and bumps of all kinds on his legs. Once these injuries have been sustained, the injured area will never fully regain its original strength. A sprained tendon, for instance, will never be as strong after recovery as it was before injury.

Previous injuries are also likely to cause recurrent problems. Injuries to the soft tissue, such as thoroughpins and windgalls, or torn or damaged muscles and ligaments, cannot hope to promise a consistently sound performance in the future.

It is not only the legs which suffer. A horse's spine takes time to mature, and may not be fully stable until at least five, or perhaps six years of age. Imagine then the harm of regularly jumping a horse too soon, when his back and quarters would be used significantly.

The two-year-old horse can be compared to a child of between eight and ten. How would we expect such a child to cope with the pressures of a young horse in training, or, more significantly, would we even try such a thing?

KEY POINTS

- The most successful way of dealing with youngsters of any age is to adopt a system of punishment and reward. Remember, however, that the misuse of punishment in early training is one of the worst errors that you can make.
- The education of the horse starts when he is still a foal.
- By the time a foal is weaned, he should accept: having the headcollar (halter) fitted without fuss; having his feet picked up and attended to; being groomed; being led and being caught.
- By the time the horse becomes a yearling, he should have learned: stable manners; simple voice commands; to be tied up without pulling back and to accept being rugged up.
- Short, regular sessions will show the most improvement.
- Routines provide stability, which will ensure the horse's happiness.
- The horse must be provided with a suitably balanced diet, relevant to each stage of his growth.
- The youngster which is started too young is more likely to develop stress injuries.

26 A horse which shows potential as a racehorse may sell for large sums of money in the sale ring, although this is of course no guarantee of success

3

BASIC REQUIREMENTS

Bitting

Bitting is the term used to describe putting a bit in the horse's mouth for the first time, and it is a very important stage. If you have bred your own horse, bitting should take place as part of his early handling and education as a yearling. If you acquire a youngster which has not had any pre-training, he should be bitted and accustomed to tack before loose schooling commences.

A snaffle bit should always be used for early training, and there are many different types in common use. A mullen-mouth snaffle is a very mild bit, while some trainers use a specially made mouthing bit which has 'keys' attached: this is to encourage the horse to salivate and so to accept the bit more readily **(fig. 9)**. This type of bit is dispensed with once the horse starts work. Other trainers simply use an ordinary, thick, jointed snaffle from the start, usually with cheekpieces to prevent the bit from being pulled through the horse's mouth **(fig. 10)**.

Fig. 9 Two types of bit often used for bitting. *(Top)* A mullen-mouth snaffle is especially useful for a horse which is very sensitive. *(Bottom)* A mouthing bit with keys is often used to encourage the horse to salivate

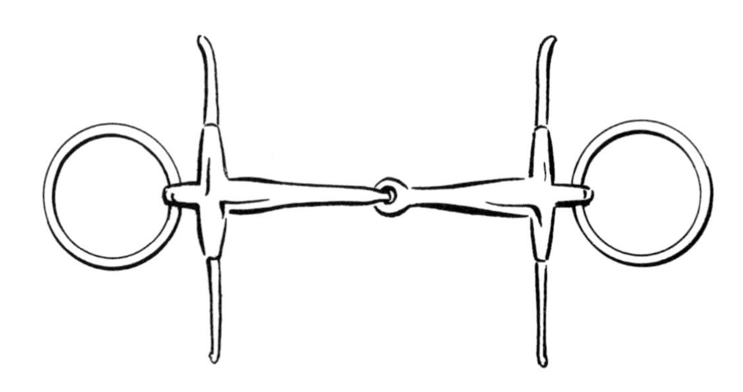

Fig. 10 A fulmer snaffle suits many horses throughout their training, many trainers use it for mouthing, as it cannot be pulled through the mouth once it is in place

Whatever snaffle bit you decide to use, it is vital that it is the correct size for the horse's mouth, and that, once in place, it is properly adjusted. The bit should sit comfortably in the corners of the mouth, just wrinkling the lips slightly, without pulling on them. This is achieved by shortening or lengthening the cheekpieces as necessary.

The width of the bit is also very important. If it is too wide, the joint will fall too low in the mouth and may bang on the horse's front teeth, and possibly bruise the corners of the mouth. This would also allow the horse to put his tongue over the bit. If, on the other hand, the bit is too narrow, it will pinch the corners of the mouth. This is not only uncomfortable for the horse, but will encourage him to lift his head to try to ease the pain, and so evade the bit.

There are two ways of bitting for the first time. One is to fasten the bit to the headcollar (halter); the other is to use the bridle straight away.

Bitting with a headcollar (halter)

To use this method, fasten the bit to the right side of the headcollar with an adjustable strap **(27)**. Then, standing with the horse's head over your shoulder, your left hand holding the bit and your right hand on the horse's nose, slide the bit into the horse's mouth and fasten it on the left side of the headcollar **(28)** and **(29)**. Encourage the horse to open his mouth, and take the bit, by sliding your thumb into the corner of his mouth. Before bitting for the first time, it is often helpful to give the horse a piece of apple to ensure that he has a moist mouth. Putting liquid molasses on to the bit also makes the whole experience a great deal more pleasant for the horse.

The well-handled horse does not usually pose any problems at this stage, and will accept the bit quite readily **(30)**. It is important not to allow him to throw his head around, although he will inevitably try to raise it away from you. The whole process should be swift, so that – before the horse has time to think about what is going on – the bit is securely in place.

Bitting with a bridle

If you use a bridle from the start, you have extra leather to hold, but the process is the same. Stand in the same manner as described with headcollar (halter) bitting, and hold the bridle cheekpieces in your right hand, resting on the horse's nose. Slip the bit into his mouth, swiftly place the headband over the horse's ears, and fasten the throat lash and noseband.

The disadvantage of using a bridle initially is that you have to slip it over the horse's ears and fiddle with buckles. If your horse is at all head-shy, or a little nervous, you should accustom him to having a bridle placed over his ears and the noseband fastened before you attempt to bit him. At all costs, you should try to ensure that the horse does not become afraid and so start to throw his head around. This may result in the bit banging his teeth, and a horse which resists being bitted in the future.

Once your horse has been bitted and is working on the lunge or in long reins, you may find that he will go better in one bit than in another. Do not be in a hurry to experiment with bits, however, unless the results you are getting with a particular bit are less than satisfactory.

If a horse does not go well in a jointed snaffle, it is usually worth trying a straight-bar snaffle, and vice versa, rather than changing to a different type of jointed snaffle. Rubber or mullen-mouth snaffles also offer an alternative, especially to a horse who is very sensitive. Once you have found a bit which suits your horse well, you should stick to it.

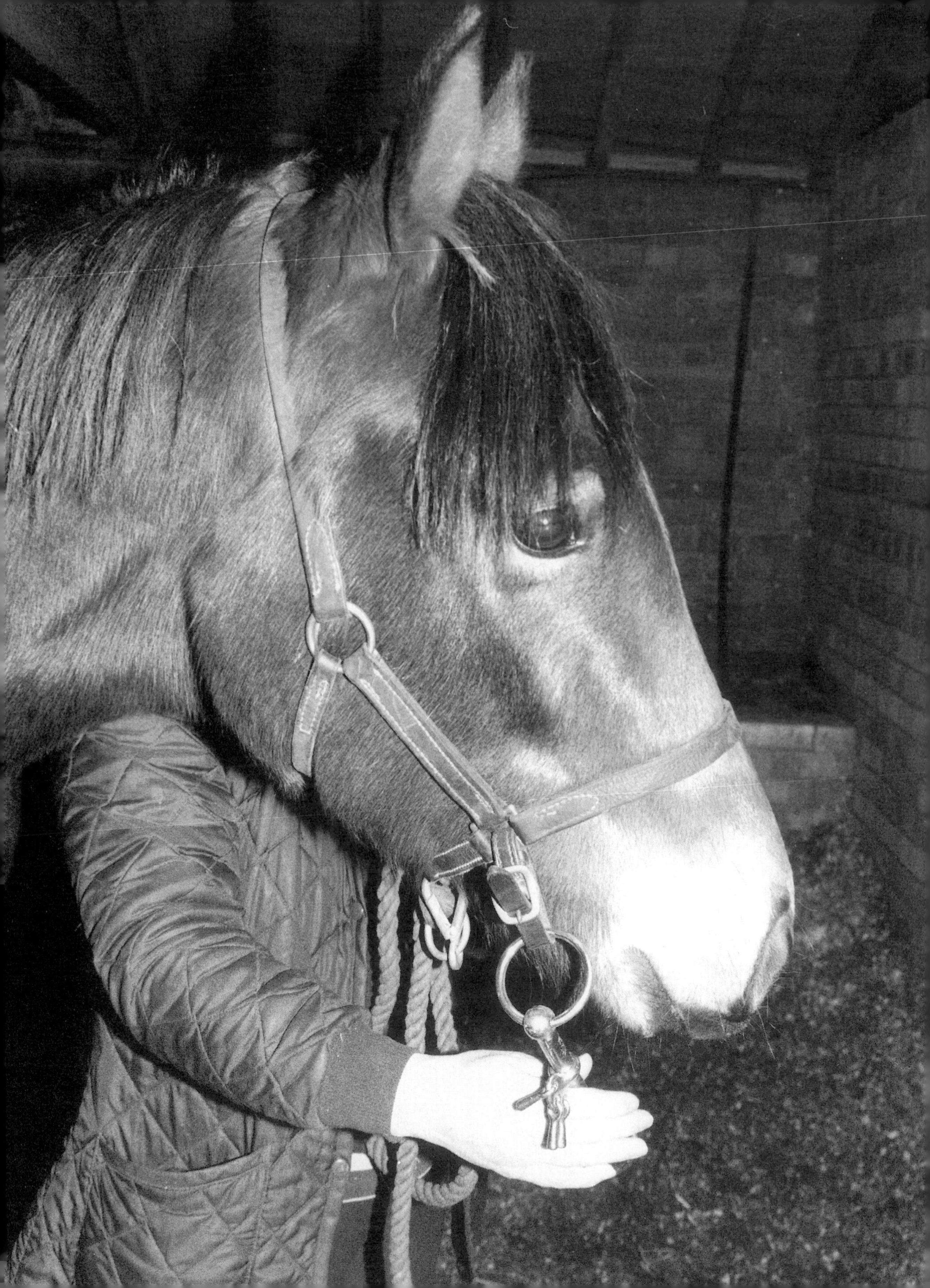

27 *(Left)* Fasten the bit to the right side of the headcollar (halter) using an adjustable strap

28 *(Right)* Hold the horse's head with your right hand and encourage him to take the bit into his mouth

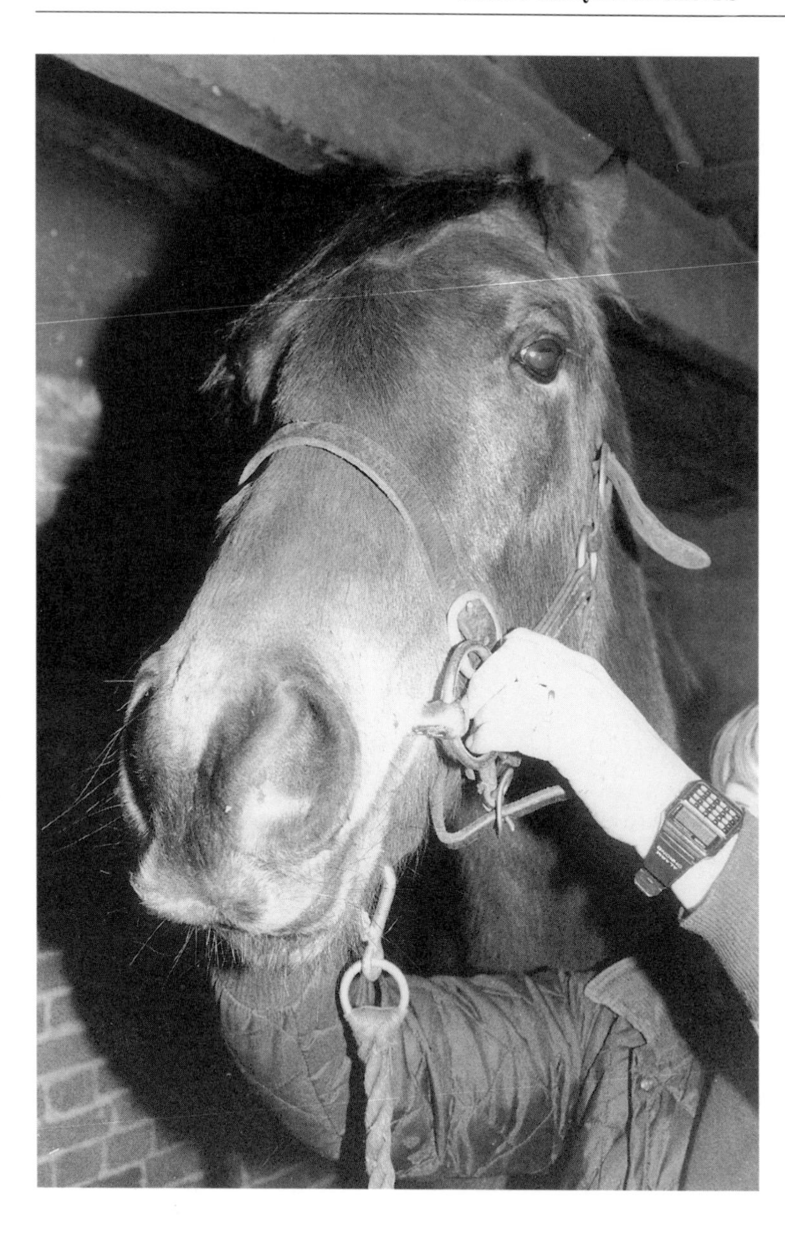

29 *(Left)* Once the bit is in his mouth, fasten it to the left side of the headcollar with another adjustable strap

30 *(Right)* The well-handled horse will normally accept the bit quite readily

Introducing the roller/ training surcingle

If your youngster has already been rugged up or accustomed to equipment at an early age, this stage will not be necessary, as he will already be accustomed to the feel of something around his middle. If he has not already been rugged up, however, then this is the next thing which needs to be accepted, before saddling takes place. The roller/training surcingle should always have a pad beneath it to prevent any damage to the spine.

Like bitting, this should pose few problems for the well-handled youngster. If you have someone to help you, ask them to hold the horse. If you are on your own, you will have to keep hold of the lead rope and proceed slowly and carefully. Do *not* tie up the horse.

Start by showing the youngster the

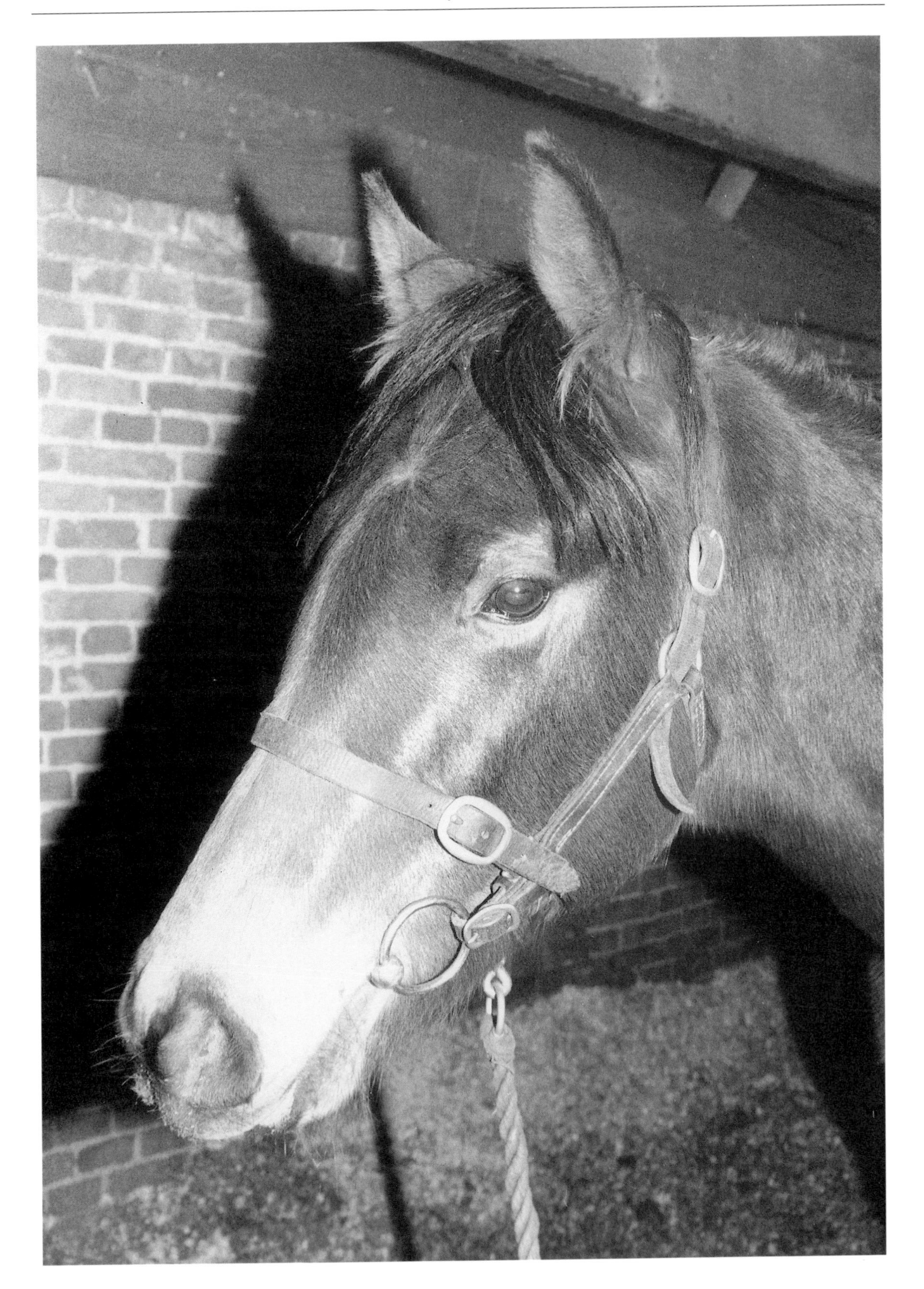

roller/training surcingle in your hands, and allow him to sniff it and to have a good look **(31)**. Then fold in half, with the buckle end on the top. Position yourself on the horse's near side, level with the withers. Gently position the roller in place behind the withers, making sure that the horse knows it is there by rocking it gently backward and forward **(32)**.

Next, walk round to the horse's off side, unfold the roller and let the buckle end hang down. Walk back to his near side, and gently reach under his belly and take hold of it. Slowly bring the strap through to you, under the horse's belly **(33)**. Do up the buckle gently until it is secure but not tight **(34)**. Gauge your horse's reaction, and allow him to to accept the feel of the roller. Then gently tighten it, one hole at a time, until it is secure enough not to slip.

The horse will probably accept the fitting without making a fuss. It is when he moves and feels the pressure on his belly that he may jump about, so be prepared. Walk the horse around the stable or school, and then allow him to go loose for a few minutes. Once he appears to have accepted the roller, carefully remove it, making sure that the buckles do not bang on his legs. Repeat the exercise every day for a few days, and frequently thereafter.

31 *(Below)* Allow the horse to see the roller (training surcingle) that is to be placed on to his back

32 *(Top right)* Gently position it in place behind the withers

33 *(Bottom right)* Slowly bring the strap up under the belly

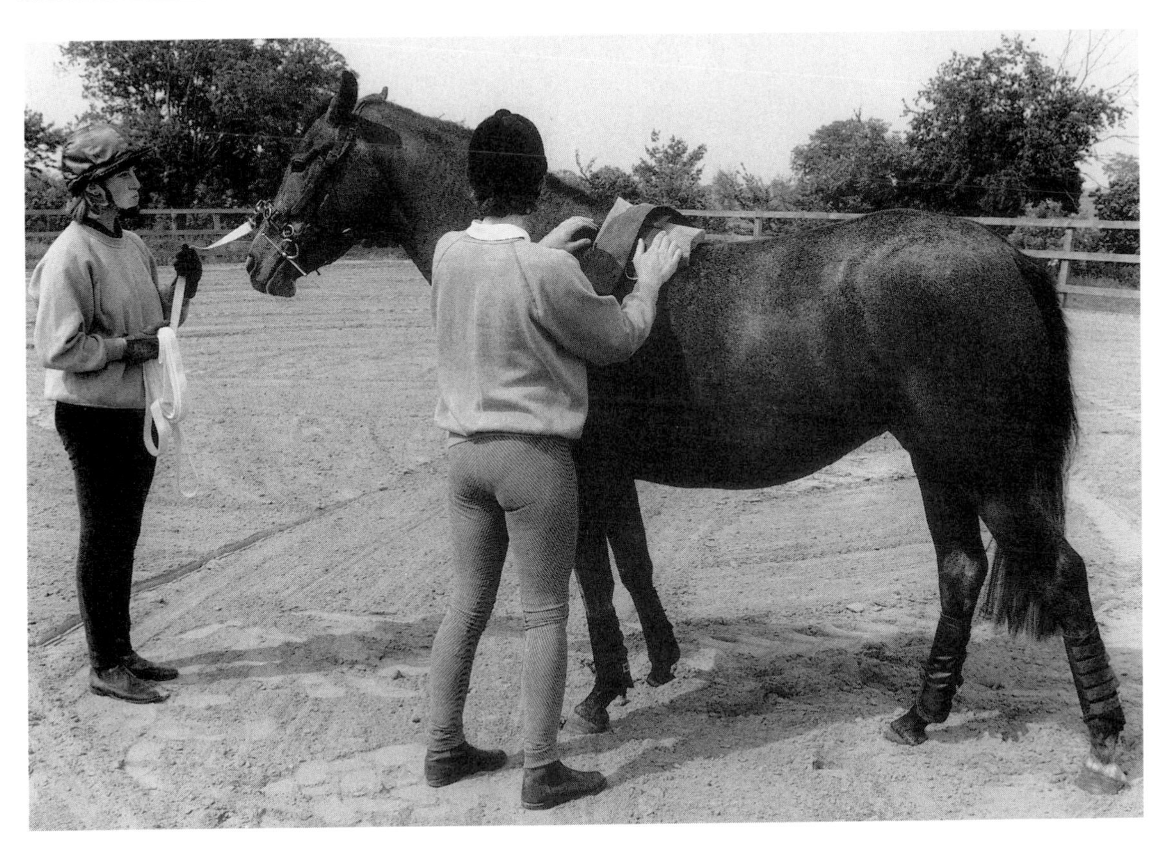

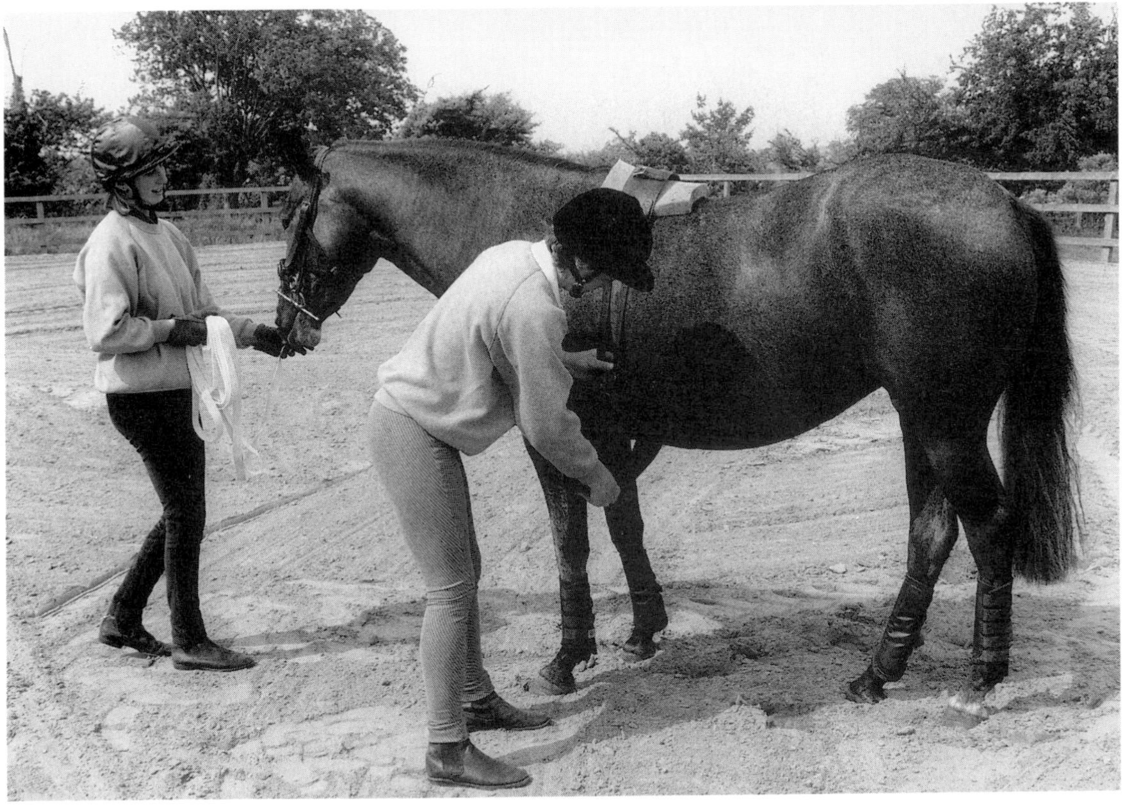

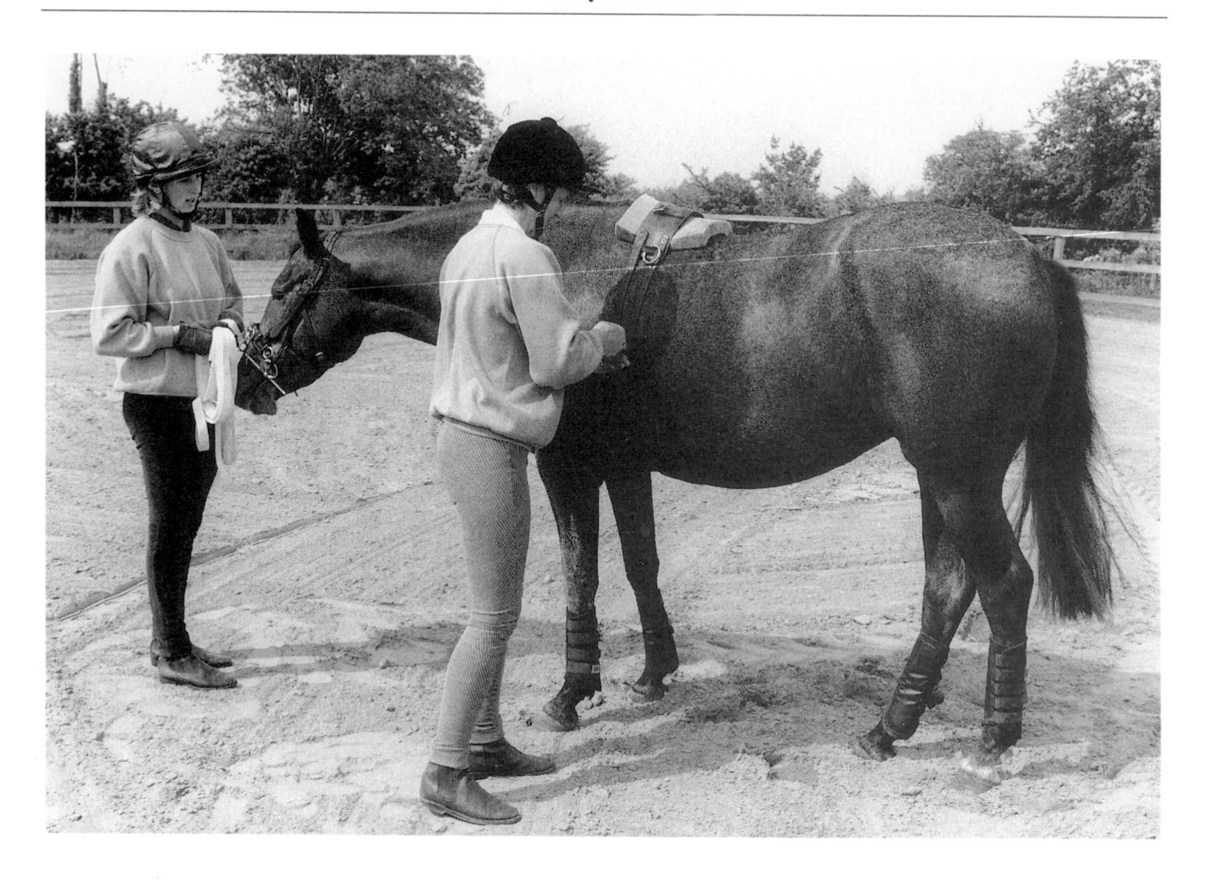

34 Gently tighten the strap, one hole at a time, until it is secure enough not to slip

35 *(Right)* Show the rug to the horse

Rugging up

Rugging up is not a basic requirement to enable the horse to be started, but it is another activity to which the horse needs to become accustomed. More people are now appreciating that stabling horses, especially youngsters, is not the best way of keeping them in good health. It is because of the problems caused by stabling – such as dust allergies, which often result in chronic obstructive pulmonary disease (COPD), and the development of vices such as wind-sucking and weaving – that youngsters are far better off living out.

It therefore makes sense to accustom the horse to a rug at an early stage, so that he can be afforded more protection from harsh weather if necessary than a shelter alone can supply, yet still retain his freedom.

For the youngster which has been rollered, rugging is simply the next step. It is a sensible precaution, when rugging for the first time, to use an old, lightweight sheet. This will be easy to manoeuvre, and will not be too great a loss should it become ripped, in the unlikely event of the horse trying to pull the rug off.

Have the rug prepared, so that it is folded from the back forwards. This will enable you to place it over the horse's quarters with the minimum of fuss. Show the rug to the horse, letting him sniff and nuzzle it **(35)**. Once he shows no signs of being wary of the rug, place it gently – still folded – over his withers, making sure not to flap it about **(36)**.

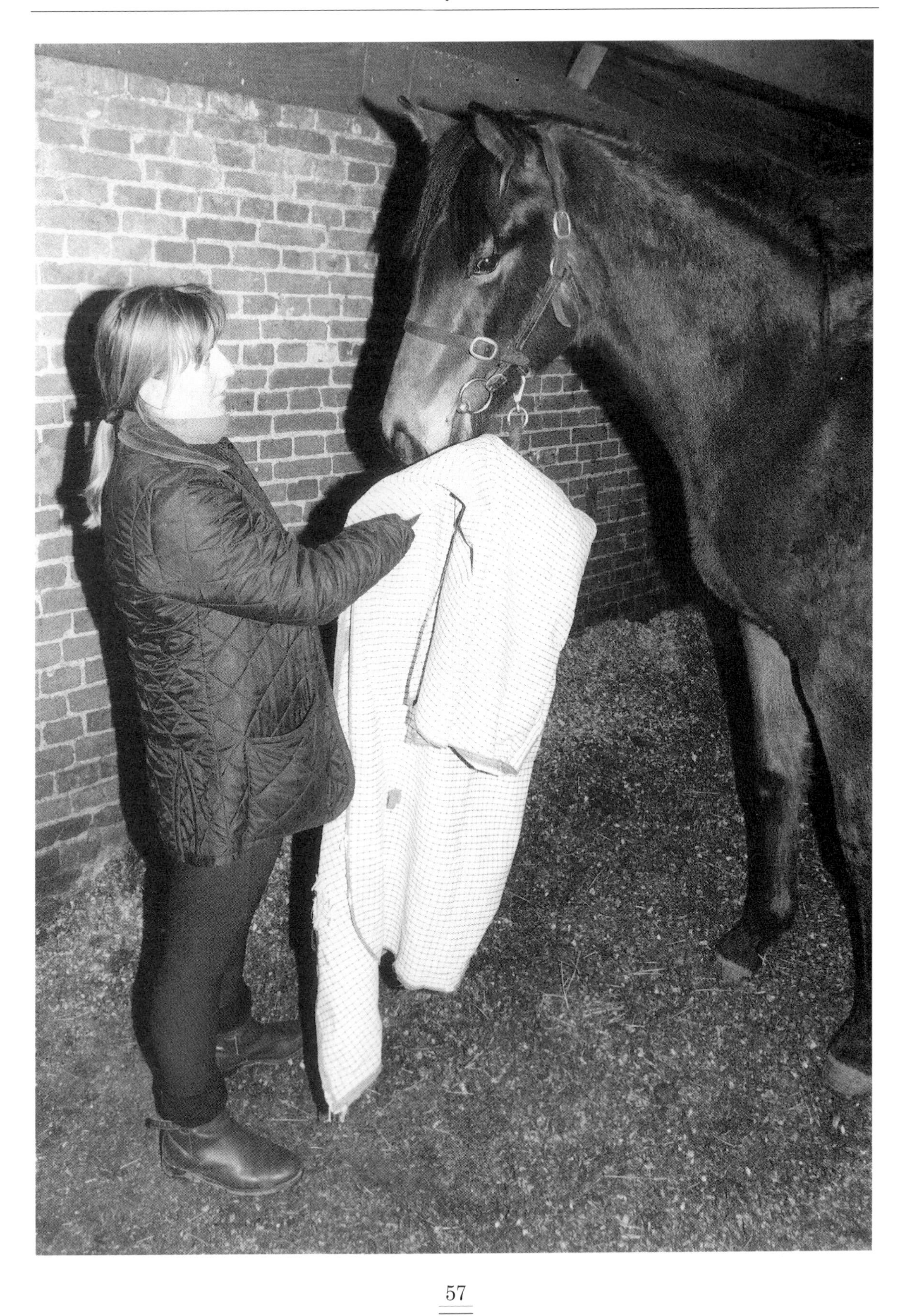

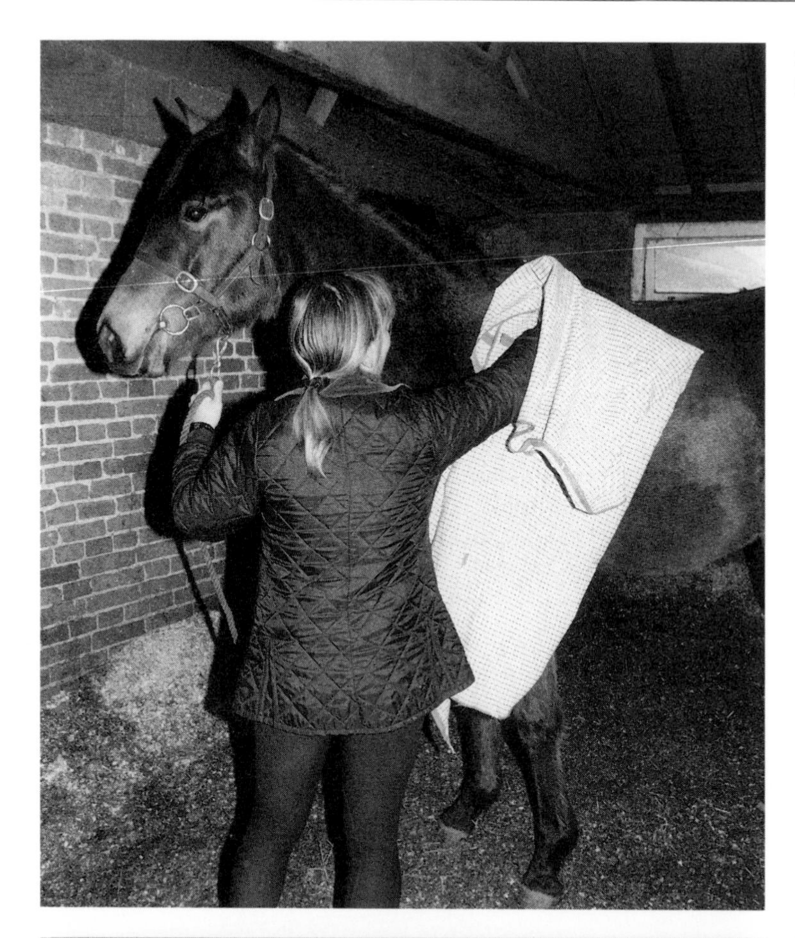

36 Gently place the rug, still folded, over his withers

37 Work from the front backwards, by firstly fastening the chest strap

Proceed slowly, and work from the front backwards, firstly by fastening the chest strap **(37)**. Then unfold the rug backwards, until it is in place over the quarters **(38)**. Put on the roller/training surcingle (an act to which the horse has already become accustomed), and secure it **(39)**. Do not use a sheet with a filet string (rump strap) at this stage, as it may annoy the horse, or become caught up in his tail if you have to remove the rug quickly. Allow the horse some moments of freedom to become used to the feel of it on him while walking around his stable **(40)**.

If, as with bitting and rollering, you have to attempt rugging up without an assistant, it is a good idea to put a bit into the horse's mouth first to give him something to think about other than what you are doing. This also lets the horse know that another training session is in hand, and therefore helps with discipline. If you bit the horse first, you should still attach the lead rope to the headcollar (halter) or noseband, not the bit, and, as before, do not tie the horse up, but keep hold of the rope yourself. Alternatively, tie a haynet in front of him to focus his attention elsewhere and to keep his head forward.

Many big yards will advise against attempting such tasks on your own, but all of these preliminary requirements are fairly easily accomplished without help if you take your time. Bear in mind that, in your favour, you have a horse which is used to you and your voice, and is in familiar surroundings. You are therefore already halfway to accomplishing these tasks, as your horse trusts you. You are not under pressure to accomplish everything quickly, and can take as long as the horse needs to accept one lesson before moving on to another.

38 Unfold the rug backwards until it is in place over the horse's quarters

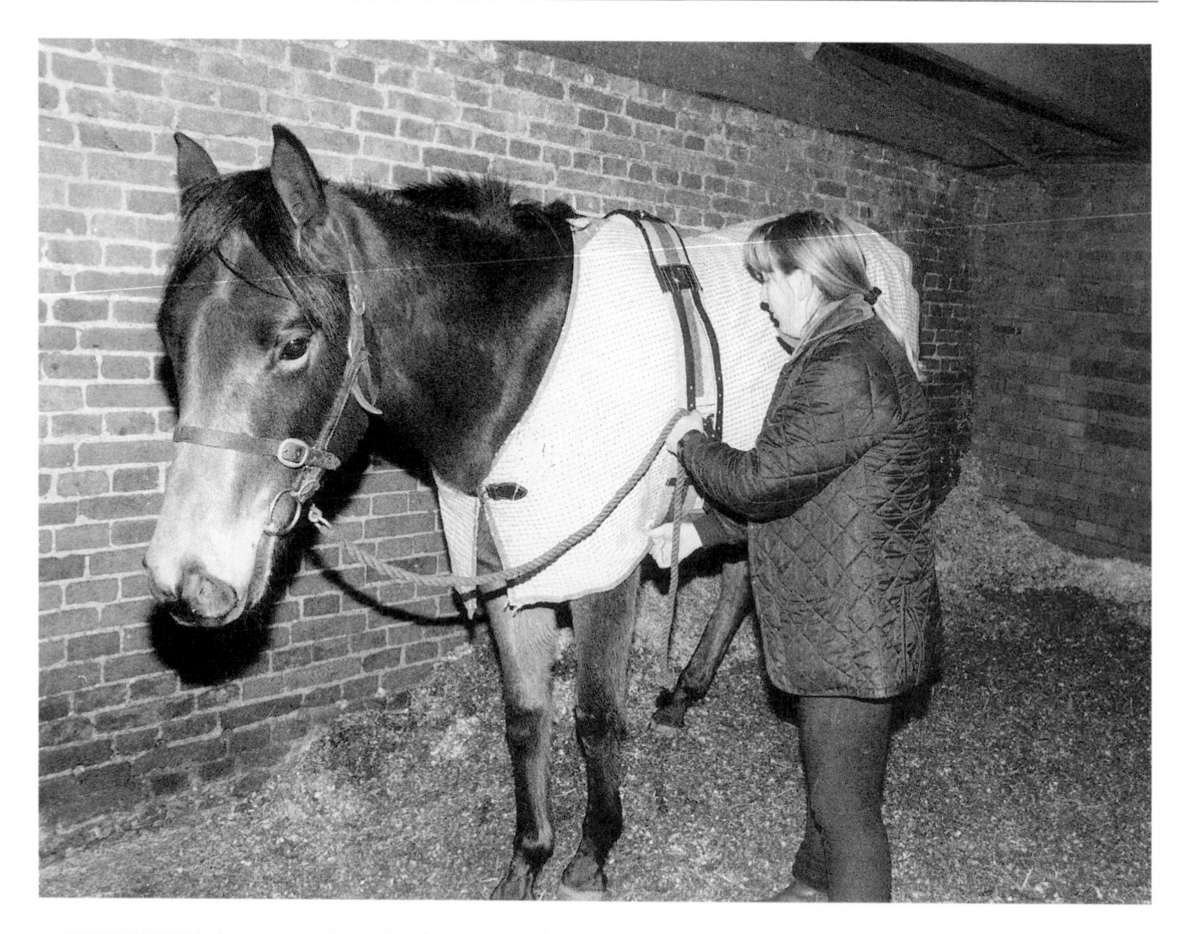

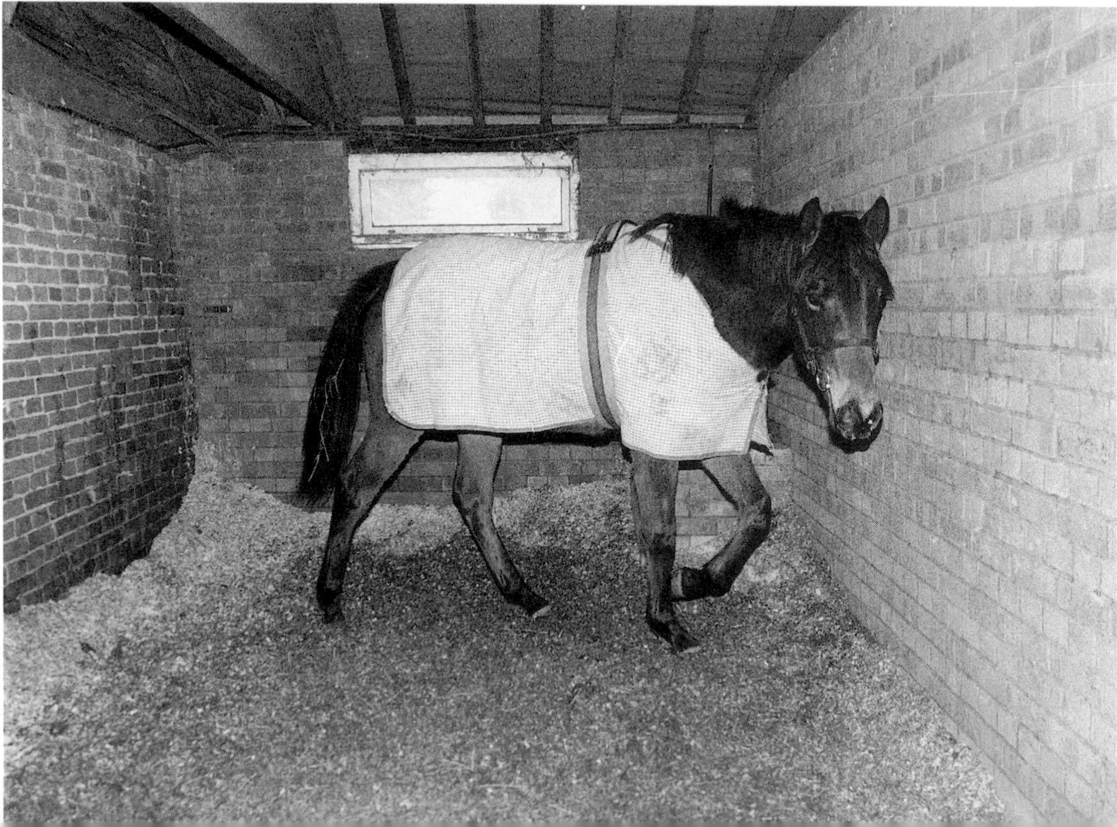

39 *(Top left)* Put on the roller and secure it

40 *(Bottom left)* Allow the horse to walk around to become used to the feel of the rug. Note how easily this youngster – which had genuinely not been rugged before – accepts the rug without fuss

Facilities

The working area

The working area that is available to you may not be purpose-built, but – although people will tell you that you should only start your young horse in an indoor school – most of us have to make the best of the

BASIC EQUIPMENT

Although there are correct items of equipment for each stage of training, it is unlikely that the newcomer will want to purchase the 'whole kit' for one horse alone. There is room for some improvisation, but there are a number of basic items which should be used in the interests of safety and comfort for the horse. Those needed to take the horse through the stages from loose schooling to backing are as follows.

- **A headcollar (halter) with lead rope:** this should be well-fitting and in good repair.
- **A plain snaffle bridle:** this should be the correct size for the horse, supple and well-kept, with no loose stitching. The bit should be well-fitting and made of stainless steel.
- **A roller/training surcingle with side rings:** this should have enough adjustment so that it will fit securely. It should be in good repair, as it may have to take a good deal of strain.
- **A lungeing cavesson:** there are various types of lungeing cavesson on the market. The overall strength of the construction and of the leather itself is vital. It is also essential that it fits the horse snugly, as, if it is too large, it will slip around and may come into contact with the horse's eyes. (see page 74 for advice on fitting the cavesson.)
- **An all-purpose saddle:** this needs to be fitted to the individual horse and should be kept supple by regular use of saddle soap.
- **Protective boots or bandages, including knee boots:** these should afford adequate protection should the horse strike into himself, and should offer a degree of support (see **fig. 31** on page 121). It may be preferable to use washable boots if you are working the horse outdoors.
- **Two lunge reins:** these should be approximately 9 m (30 ft) each in length. Whether fastened by means of a clip or a buckle, each rein should have a swivel attachment to allow for freedom of movement.
- **A pair of side reins:** these should be adjustable enough to allow muscular freedom of the back and neck. Some are made of plain leather, while others have an elasticated section or rubber rings, which 'give' a little.
- **A lungeing whip:** this needs to be long enough overall so that it is never shorter than the distance between the trainer and the horse on full lunge. In other words, the tip of the thong should be able to touch the horse should this be necessary. The balance of the whip is also important, and this must be related to the person using it. In general, a man with a strong wrist will need a heavier whip than a smaller woman.

You may already have much of this equipment, or may be able to borrow it, and it is unnecessary to buy expensive purpose-made equipment such as breaking rollers or long reins at this stage.

facilities that we have. One important consideration should be the size of the working area, and this needs to be related to the activity. It is far easier to loose school without the aid of an assistant, for example, in an area no bigger than 20 × 40 m (65 × 130 ft). If the area is any larger, you will not be able to keep the horse out on the track should he decide to come in.

It is possible to lunge a horse in a larger area, as it is the length of rein used and your position which determine where the horse will go. However, it is much easier to lunge in an area approximately 20 m (65 ft) in diameter, as the horse will not have the opportunity of pulling away from you.

Wide-open spaces can be a little frightening or exciting for a young horse, so the area needs to be fenced, ideally with a solid wooden wall high enough to discourage any thoughts of jumping out. The horse will then be able to balance himself better and will concentrate more on your requests, rather than on what is going on around him. Failing this, or if a makeshift school is needed at some time, solid wooden hurdles or straw bales can be erected to form a safe working area. Hurdles should not have feet which will protrude into the working area, and they should slant outward.

41 Whatever the schooling area, it must be well looked after

Provided that it is a suitable size, your school could be an indoor school, a purpose-built, all-weather, outdoor ménage, or a suitable corner of a field, securely partitioned off. An indoor school does provide the most advantages, the more obvious being shelter from adverse weather and a dry surface, but few people have access to one for the regular sessions that a young horse needs. As in early training, the working area should become a familiar place to the horse, and so it is best to start training sessions where they will always take place.

Once the horse is lungeing under control, however, it is beneficial to lunge him in a different area, to make sure that he will be fully obedient to your requests when in a new place or when there are other distractions.

Another consideration to be given to the working area is the going, which should neither be hard nor have too deep a surface. If you are schooling in a corner of a field, you will need to ensure that the going does not become too heavy after a lot of rain, as this will cause great strain on the youngster's legs. The surface must not be at all slippery, so you may need to put down woodshavings or sand, depending on the time of year **(41)**. It also needs to be flat and level. Young horses often find difficulty in keeping their balance, even without the hindrance of a sloping surface.

Once you have bitted and rollered your horse and prepared a suitable working area, your three-year-old can be started safely.

Playtime

If your horse is stabled, another facility essential to his well-being is an area in which to turn him out. All youngsters are playful, and if he is not afforded the benefit of playing and kicking about out in the field, he will do so in training sessions instead. The paddock should be well-fenced and well-drained, as it is quite common for youngsters to strain or injure themselves if they are left to gallop about in boggy conditions.

KEY POINTS

- Bitting is the term used to describe putting a bit in the horse's mouth for the first time.
- Whatever snaffle bit you choose, it is vital that it is the correct size for the horse's mouth.
- Rollering, like bitting, should pose few problems for the well-handled youngster.
- When training youngsters, there are basic items of equipment which should be used in the interests of safety and comfort for the horse.
- Although an indoor school or all-weather ménage may be the ideal place to start a youngster, it is perfectly in order to use a secure corner of a field.
- It is essential to the stabled horse's well-being that he has a suitable 'play area' in which he can be turned out safely.
- The owner or trainer who has taken the time to bit and roller his horse gently, and who has prepared a suitable working area, is one who can start his horse safely.

Part 2

TRAINING TO RIDE

4

TRAINING PROCEDURE

Training from the ground

When starting a horse's training in earnest, there are three methods of schooling from the ground which can be employed. Some trainers prefer to use only one or two of the methods, while others prefer to progress from one method to another as training advances. Indeed, there is a natural progression between the methods, and one can benefit another if carried out at the appropriate stage of training.

The three methods are *loose schooling*, *lungeing* and *long reining*. Although each is an art in itself, becoming reasonably proficient at each – enough to teach a young horse the basics, at least – is not beyond the bounds of any patient, attentive owner.

THE STAGES OF TRAINING

Starting a horse can be categorized into four separate stages.

- Early education: the pre-training stage from handling the foal to the three-year old (as outlined in Chapter 2).
- Training from the ground (this is divided into further sections, as explained in this chapter. Detailed information on these training methods is given in Chapters 5 and 6).
- Backing and riding away.
- Following-up: elementary training.

Loose schooling

Loose schooling is particularly beneficial as a starting point. It educates the horse to voice commands, and allows him to become accustomed to the trainer's requests, in a very natural way **(fig. 11)**. The horse does not immediately feel restricted by the use of tack and lunge reins, and his still-maturing joints are not subjected to unnecessary stresses and strains, often inadvertently caused by human restraint on the lunge. Once the horse is loose schooling in a relaxed manner, he can be accustomed to the equipment which will be used for lungeing.

The aim of loose schooling is to have the horse increasing or decreasing pace in a relaxed manner by the use of your voice and body position. The horse needs to be taught that, if you position yourself behind him, at a certain angle, you wish him to move forward or increase pace, depending on the verbal commands also given. Conversely, if you position yourself on an angle slightly in front of him, it means that you require him to decrease pace or to stop, again aided by verbal commands.

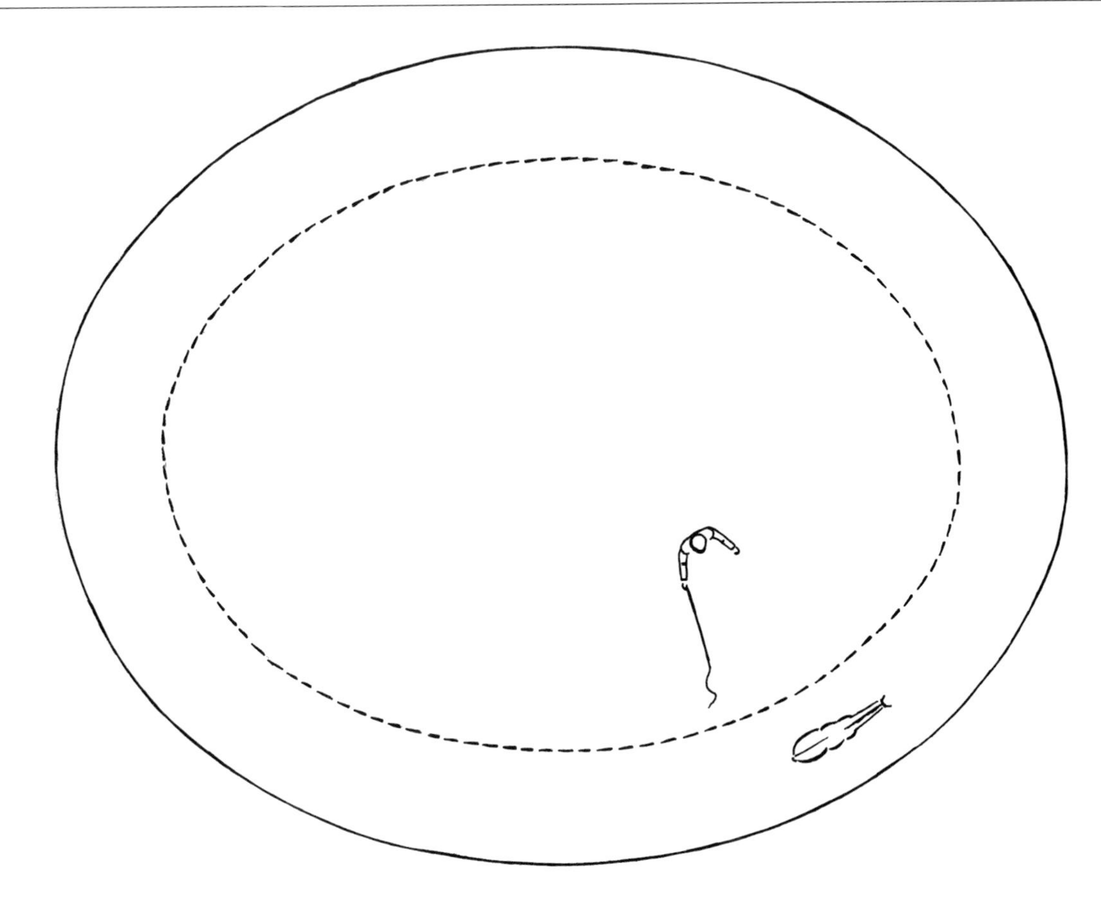

Fig. 11 Loose schooling – without any restriction on the horse – is a very good and natural way of preparing him for lungeing

Lungeing

Lungeing progresses from loose schooling, as the horse will have already learned voice commands and will be used to you driving him forward around the school with the aid of a lungeing whip. Lungeing goes further, however, in that you have greater control over your horse.

You can give him the 'feel' of being driven purposely from behind (as, later, the rider's legs and seat will do), and to being restrained in front (to simulate the pressure that the rider will give on the reins). This will develop him both mentally and physically, without having to put weight on his back **(fig. 12)**.

Both loose schooling and lungeing can also be very beneficial when teaching the horse to jump (see pages 138–43).

Long reining

Long reining allows still greater control over the horse. It is an excellent way of teaching him discipline, without being ridden **(fig. 13)**. Through the long reins, attached to the bit, the horse learns to respond to simple aids that the rider will give through the rein, and through the contact of the long reins on his side, he learns the 'feel' of aids given on his sides through the rider's legs. As a result, a horse which has been long reined well will be far more likely to respond quickly to a rider on his back when the time comes.

Each method of training employed from the ground can therefore be structured to

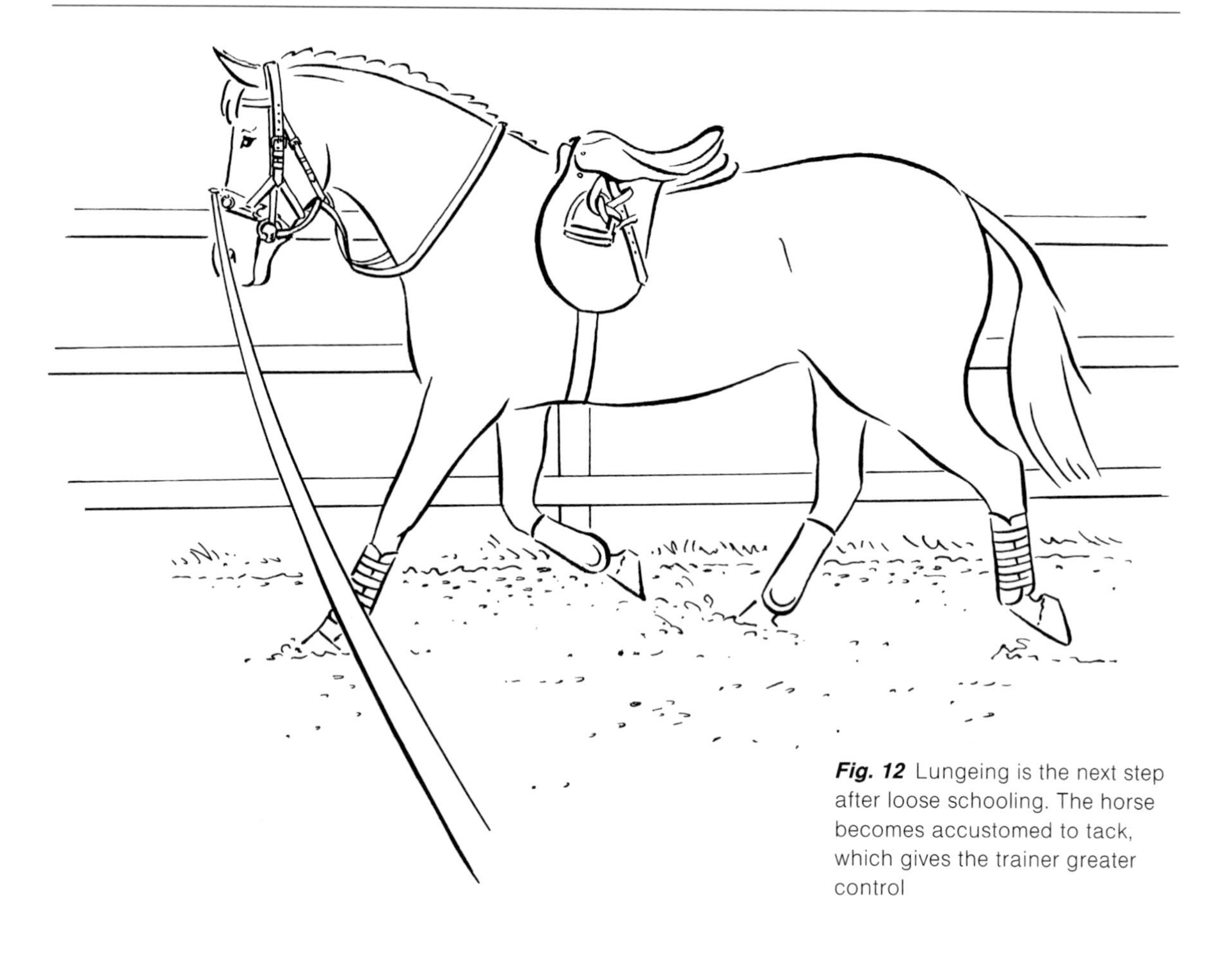

Fig. 12 Lungeing is the next step after loose schooling. The horse becomes accustomed to tack, which gives the trainer greater control

progress from one stage to the next, which will be of great benefit when it comes to backing the horse and riding him away. Through the training stages the horse will develop his muscles, will become more supple with an increase in joint flexion, and – because he will learn to engage his hind legs more productively – will show an overall improvement in balance and rhythm.

It is with this knowledge in mind that you will work through the principles and methods of each stage with your young horse. It should be recognized, however, that each stage is a 'complete' method in itself, and will be used at various times throughout the horse's career. None is an infallible method to producing perfectly disciplined, unridden youngsters; yet, by working methodically through the various stages, your aim will be to produce a well-balanced horse, both mentally and physically – a horse which you can go on to ride with confidence and pleasure.

Objectives

The most important ingredient of each stage of training is time. It cannot be emphasized enough that each horse is an individual, and that each will progress at a different rate. You cannot, therefore, put a time limit on any stage or on any one aspect being taught.

While there are no timetables, however, there are aims. You should consider the training of the young horse in terms of questions and answers, which are given as requests by us and responses by the horse. You will ask the horse questions (these will be very simple at first) by the use of actions and verbal commands, and wait for the correct answers in the form of understanding and obedience. The horse which does not understand cannot obey, and so patience is your most important asset.

If the horse does not give the correct response, you must repeat your request until he does understand what is required of him. Each lesson should be clearly taught, and not until the horse has thoroughly understood the lesson should he be asked anything new.

For the youngster just being started, lessons should be kept simple and short. As a guide, approximately twenty minutes per lesson is long enough initially. It is a misconception to make the horse continue until he has got it right, as, instead of achieving the desired result, you are only likely to confuse the horse until it is

Fig. 13 Long reining progresses further still, as the horse learns to respond to simple aids that he will be given at a later stage when he is ridden

impossible for him to respond in the required way. It is far better to put the horse away after a short session, and to bring him out to try again later in the day, once he has rested.

At this stage in the horse's education – whether you are loose schooling, lungeing or long reining – your basic aim is to have the horse moving forward on command in a free and balanced outline. To accomplish this, you must begin by relaxing the horse. Once you have achieved this, your task will be a great deal easier, as the horse will be more willing to listen to your requests and will try hard to carry them out.

Your goal at this stage is to produce a horse which will behave sensibly when it comes to backing.

Disadvantages

The benefits of each training method from the ground are numerous and the disadvantages few. When problems do occur, they are likely to be the result of rushing or ignorance on the trainer's part, rather than the activity itself.

For instance, if you expect the horse to settle straight away when loose schooling, and do not allow time for him to begin to listen to your voice before issuing commands, a communication barrier will be set up. The rest of the session is therefore likely to be disastrous, and may prove to be the beginning of a very unnecessary battle.

Similarly, if you ask the horse to canter on the lunge before he is properly balanced, strain on the joints will result, and the horse will also find it difficult to cope mentally.

It is plain, then, that the biggest disadvantage to the new trainer is not necessarily lack of knowledge, but *inexperience*. It is for this reason that anyone wishing to start youngsters should endeavour to learn as much as possible of the processes involved, by watching others and by practising on older horses, before tackling their first youngster.

KEY POINTS

- There is a natural progression between loose schooling, lungeing and long reining, and one can benefit another if carried out at the appropriate stage of training.
- Loose schooling is particularly beneficial as a starting point. It educates the horse to voice commands, and allows him to become accustomed to requests by the trainer, in a very natural way.
- Lungeing goes further than loose schooling, because it gives greater control over the horse.
- Long reining allows still greater control over the horse, and is an excellent way of teaching discipline.
- The most important ingredient of each stage of training is time; each horse is an individual and each will progress at a different rate.
- The training of the young horse should be considered in terms of questions and answers, which are given as requests by us and responses by the horse.
- The biggest disadvantage to the new trainer is not necessarily lack of knowledge, but inexperience.

5

LOOSE SCHOOLING AND LUNGEING

Loose-schooling in preparation for lungeing

Loose schooling is used at each end of the horse's early education: firstly, in preparation for lungeing, and secondly, in preparation for jumping, once the horse has been successfully backed.

In the preparation for lungeing there are two stages to loose schooling, both of which can be most enjoyable for horse and trainer. The first stage is letting the horse loose, and the second is familiarizing him with the training equipment to be used later on.

Loose schooling: stage 1

The first session

The first thing to do is to prepare the school. This is one stage of training where there *must* be a solid fence all around. Natural hedges are excellent 'solid' fences, and, if a corner of a hedged field is used, this leaves only two sides of the school to be suitably fenced.

When loose schooling without the aid of an assistant, it is very difficult (as discussed on page 62) to control the horse in an area larger than 20 by 40 m (65 × 130 ft) and it is foolish to attempt to do so. You will therefore need either to work in an area no bigger than this, or to employ the aid of a willing assistant from the beginning.

Position four or six cones around the working area, approximately 2 m ($6\frac{1}{2}$ ft) from the school wall, to give the horse something to go around and to encourage him on to the outside track **(fig. 14)**.

Place the lunge whip in the middle of the school, and then go and prepare your horse. Put on his protective leg boots and lead him into the school in a headcollar. Carry some pony nuts (cubes) in your pocket to offer a reward when he earns it.

Walk to the middle of the school, and gently pick up the lungeing whip. Allow the horse to see and sniff it, but do not touch him with it. The lunge whip is something that he must respect, but he should not be made afraid of it.

Lead your horse around the track on the left rein a few times from the left (near) side, holding the whip in your left hand. Hold the lash along the whip with it pointing backwards, so that it is not dragging on the floor behind you. Next, turn on to the right rein and lead your horse on his right (off) side. Although this may seem alien to you (most people always lead a horse from the near side), the aim is

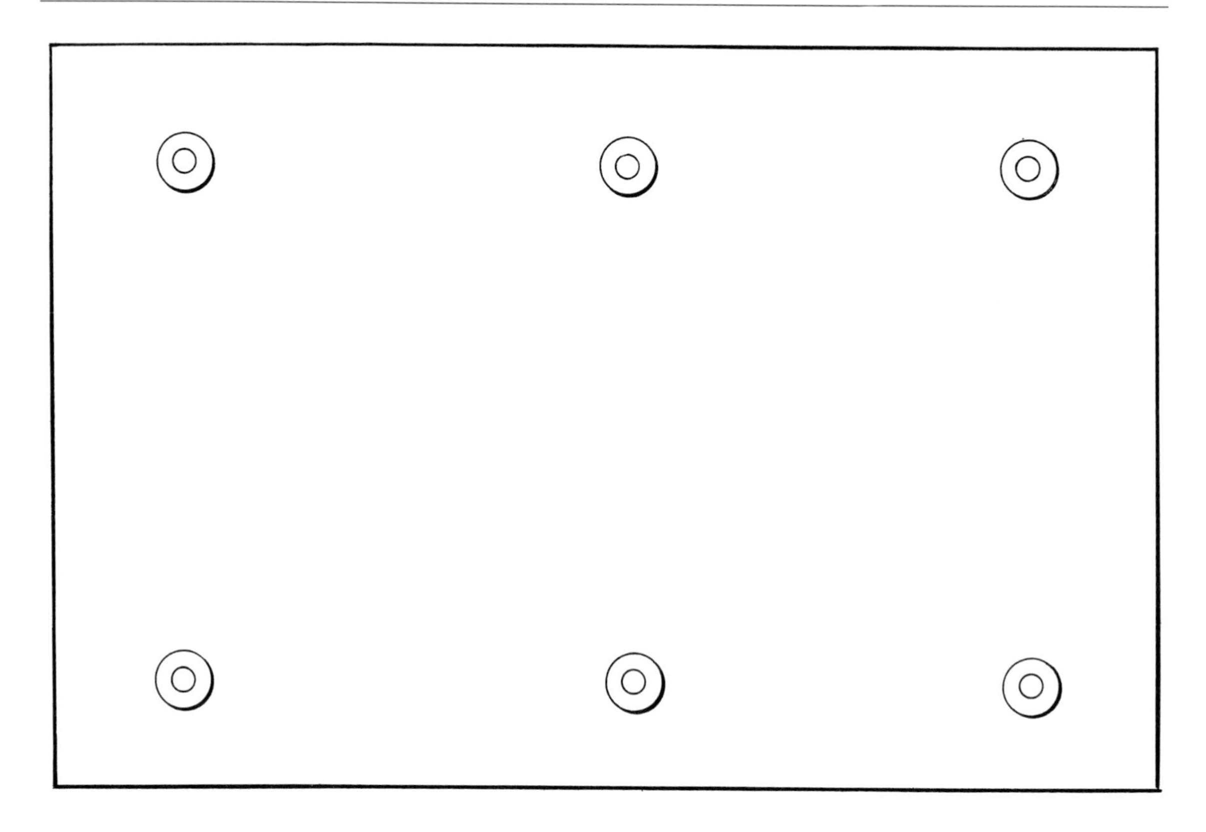

Fig. 14 The position of bollards for loose schooling

always to put yourself on the inside of the school.

Next, take your horse to the centre of the school and unclip his lead rope. Once he realizes that he is loose, he will probably trot around and kick about all over the school. Do not try to stop him, as it is here that you must wait for the horse to settle of his own accord. Talk to him all the time, but do not request anything of him.

Once the horse has settled, ask him to come to you in your usual way. Ask him to 'stand', and clip the lead rope back on. If he obliges, offer him a treat (cubes) and reward him by telling him that he is good in the way to which he is accustomed. If he ignores you or runs off playfully, let him. Simply wait for him to settle once more, and again offer a treat.

Once you have put the lead rope back on and shown the horse that you are pleased with him, lead him into the middle of the school and let him loose again. He will be less likely to plunge off this time, and now you should encourage him to walk away from you, towards the outside of the school. If he trots off, let him do so, but be ready to position yourself so as to keep him on the outside track. At first he will not understand what you want, so you will have to make your actions obvious.

Keep the horse calm at all times by using the familiar voice commands that you have already taught him, and try not to be negative in your actions or words. Remember, you are aiming to develop obedience through the association of ideas, so, if the horse trots off, encourage him by saying 'teerot', so that he associates the word with his own actions. Similarly, if he just stands still, encourage him by saying 'stand', before asking him to 'walk on'.

In this first session, try not to use the lunge whip too much, as the horse may become excitable and the results will not be as productive as they might otherwise be. Once your horse has responded to your voice, has been encouraged to move away from you to the outside of the school, and has come to you when requested and stood to be caught, the lesson has served its purpose. In any case, the lesson should only be a short one, of not more than about fifteen minutes. It is a good idea to make this first lesson early on in the morning, so that, if the horse has not responded well, you can give him another short session later on in the afternoon.

If the horse is at all hot, walk him around on the lead rein to cool him off before putting him back in his stable.

Fig. 15 The position in which the trainer moves in relation to the horse when loose schooling

Asking the horse to respond to the voice

Loose-schooling sessions should carry on each day. If the horse responds positively to your requests each time, then one or two sessions a day will be sufficient. If he becomes easily confused, however, then he will benefit from three short sessions a day.

At the beginning of the second session, repeat the previous day's lesson. Most horses need to have a little fun before they are able to settle and concentrate on your requests, but they do usually settle more quickly as time goes on.

Once settled, most horses are happy to trot on around the school at first. To keep the horse moving forward around the bollards, you should walk actively towards his quarters, keeping slightly behind his eye. The further you position yourself behind the horse's eye, the quicker he will

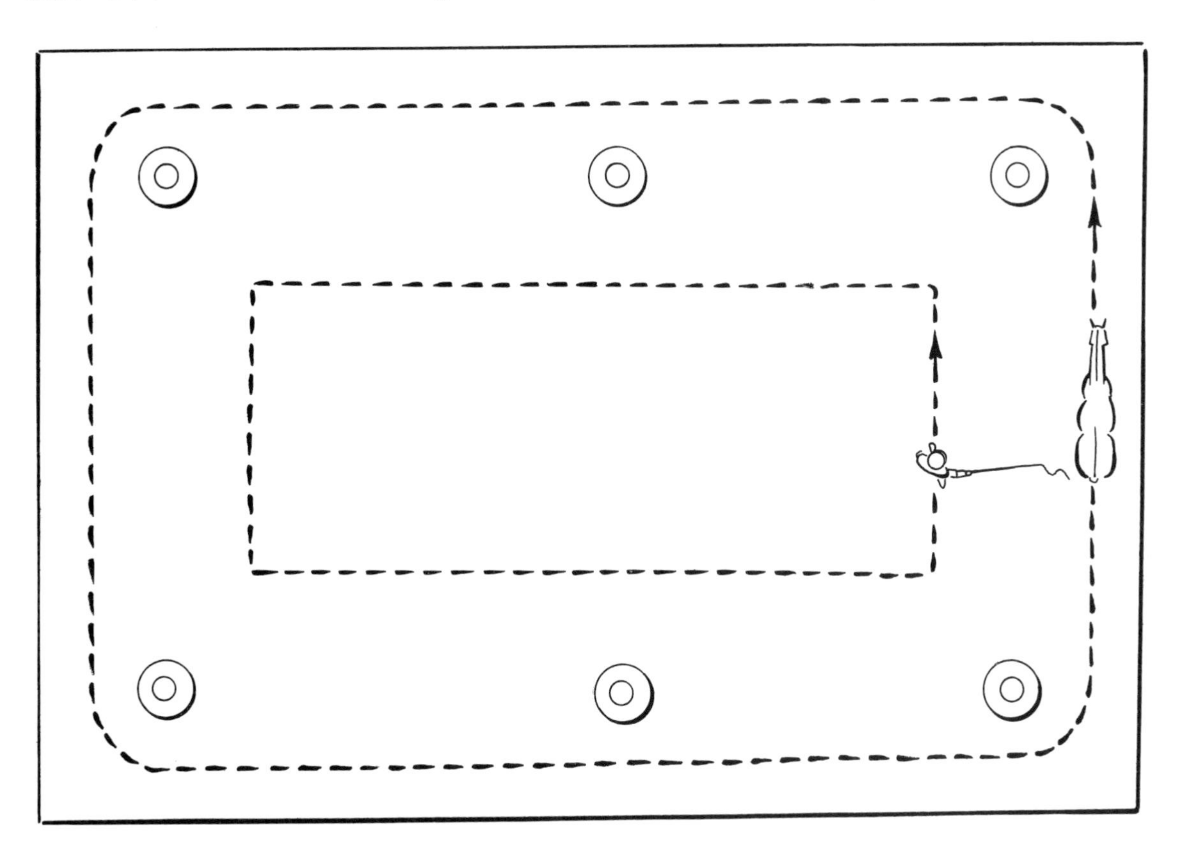

move. Aim to keep at the same angle all the way round the school, with the horse in front of you. You are aiming to get the horse to associate his actions with the voice commands you are using, so you should frequently use the word 'teerot' while he is maintaining that pace.

Once you are able to keep the horse out on the track, in whatever pace he sets, you can then try to request a change in pace. To ask the horse to slow the pace, for example, position yourself slightly in front of his eye, and repeat the word 'whooa', or whatever your word might be, as you keep walking. Once he slows to a walk, send him on in walk by repeating 'walk on', as you position yourself slightly behind his eye again **(fig. 15)**.

You will be surprised at how quickly the horse learns what is required of him, and within a week of regular sessions he will probably stand, walk, trot and canter and come to you when requested.

TIPS FOR LOOSE SCHOOLING

- Be certain of the words that you will use for each pace and for rewarding the horse, and stick to them throughout. Do not talk to the horse other than to repeat the word which you want him to associate with his present action. In this way, not only will the horse quickly learn your voice commands, but, more importantly, he will understand what response is required.
- Although the horse may learn to loose school fairly quickly, the sessions should carry on for some time, simply repeating what he has learned.
- Be sure, however, to vary what you ask each time you take the horse into the school. If in the last session, for instance, you asked him to start off on the right rein in walk and then asked him to trot on, in the next session ask him to start off on the left in walk, and then to stand before moving off again.

Loose schooling: stage 2

Once the horse is responding readily to your wishes, you can begin to introduce the equipment that you will use to lunge him. The benefit of doing so at this stage is that the horse will have already learned to trust you to a certain degree. He will also be in familiar surroundings, and you can soothe him with familiar words if he seems a little nervous.

He will already be used to wearing protective leg boots, and will have been bitted and rollered. Some people prefer to leave rollering until this stage, but there really is no benefit in doing so, and a rollered horse will accept the saddle more easily. As you will not be trying to start the horse in a matter of days, the gradual build-up will benefit those who have to start horses with very little help, or those who are starting a horse for the first time. The horse which is started gradually poses fewer problems in such circumstances.

Fitting the lungeing cavesson

The next step is to fit the lungeing cavesson. This should be the correct size for the horse, and in good repair. The lungeing cavesson has a padded nose piece which is fitted with three rings, one in the centre and one on either side, on to which the lungeing rein can be attached.

The cavesson is fitted in exactly the same way as a headcollar (halter), although it has an extra strap attached to the cheekpieces to keep them away from the horse's eyes when he is being lunged. Some cavessons also have a browband. It is easier for the first few fittings to do without this, as it means more fiddling around the horse's ears, to which he may

42 A correctly fitted lungeing cavesson

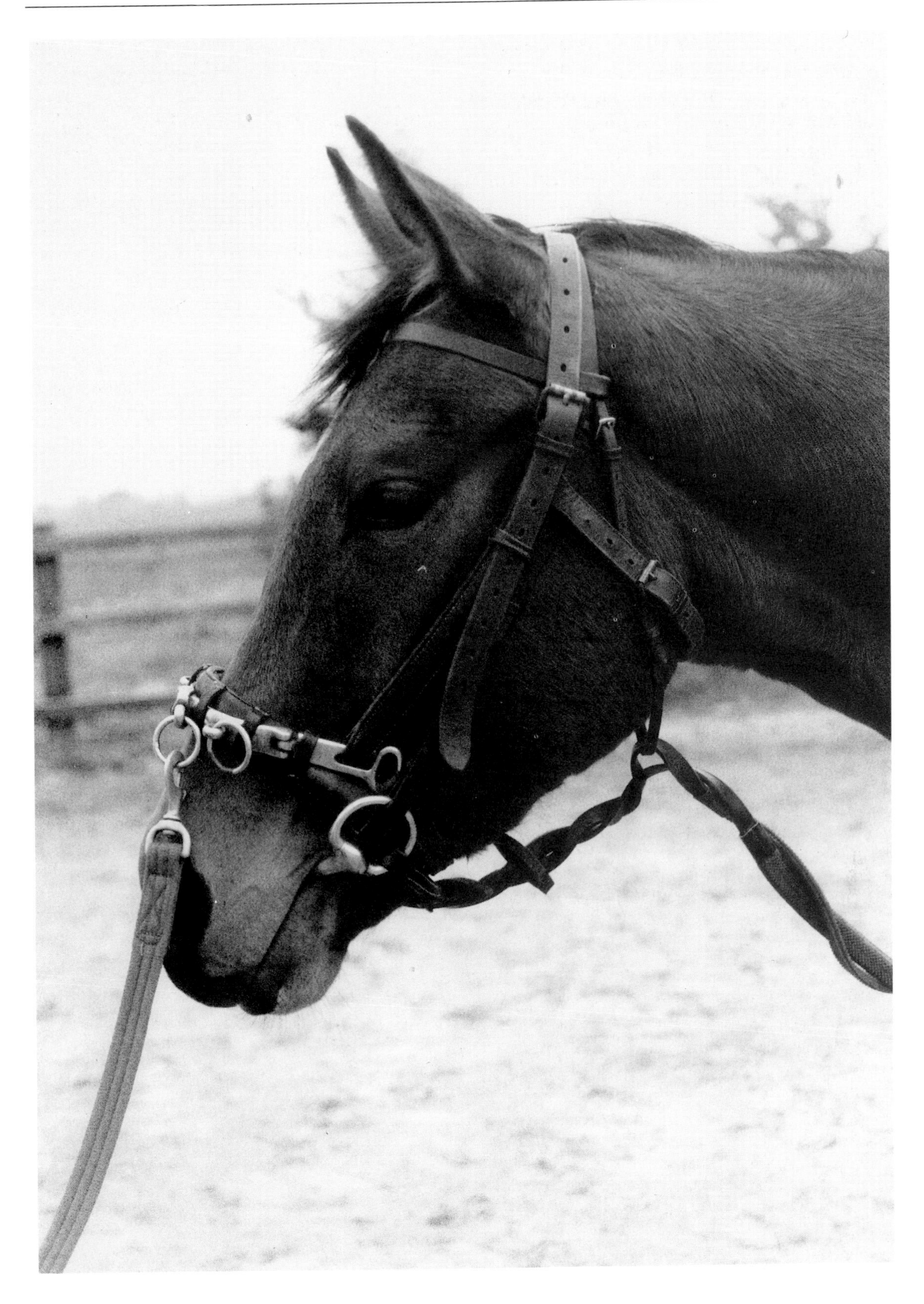

object. There is no safety risk in removing the browband, as the horse is not being lunged at this stage, and so no pressure is being put on to the cavesson.

For the first fitting, keep the headcollar (halter) on underneath, to ensure that you have hold of the horse at all times. Once the cavesson is on, you will need to adjust it so that it is a snug and comfortable fit **(42)**.

Once you have fitted the cavesson, allow your horse to go loose in the school. He may not take any notice of the cavesson, or he may throw his head around a little until he learns to accept the noise of the metal rings jingling and the extra weight on his nose. Put the cavesson on your horse each time you loose school and he will soon disregard its presence, for at this stage you are not controlling him by it.

Saddling

The next step is saddling. This is a simple procedure for the rollered horse, and is carried out in exactly the same way.

With an assistant holding the horse if possible, gently place the saddle on the horse's withers and slide it backwards until it rests naturally, immediately behind the withers **(43)**. Let the girth down, ensuring that it does not bang the horse's legs, and fasten it one hole at a time to prevent the horse from 'blowing out' **(44)**. You should also use a surcingle the first two or three times that you fit a saddle, to prevent the flaps from banging and frightening the horse if he bucks.

Once the saddle is secure, prepare yourself to walk the horse on, as again it is at this stage that the horse may take exception to the extra weight. In reality, very few horses built up so gradually give rodeo displays, and at worst may simply jump about a little. If the horse seems untroubled by the saddle, let him loose and ask him to trot on around the school a few times, before catching him up and putting him away.

The only remaining piece of equipment to which a horse needs to be accustomed are side reins. As these are not used until the horse is lungeing properly, however, they do not need to be fitted at this stage.

Lungeing

The day of the first lungeing session always seems to mark the start of 'official' training. Perhaps this is because more people lunge young horses than loose school or long rein them, or perhaps because this is the first time that you will actually 'take hold' of the horse.

Lungeing is used for five main reasons:

- as a method of training young horses, including starting them to jump
- to exercise horses which are unable for various reasons to be ridden
- to school horses, including advanced work
- for re-training spoilt horses
- to teach beginner riders

The novice trainer

Correct lungeing is a real art, and needs as much – if not more – skill than correct riding. It is, at the same time, a skill which can be learned, and which is within the scope of anyone dedicated to training youngsters. The only way to learn how to lunge is to actually do it, but it is sensible

43 The horse which has been rollered correctly normally poses few problems when it comes to saddling, but be careful not to allow the saddle to fall heavily on to his back. It should be gently rested on the withers and then slid back into place

44 The girth is tightened slowly, one hole at a time

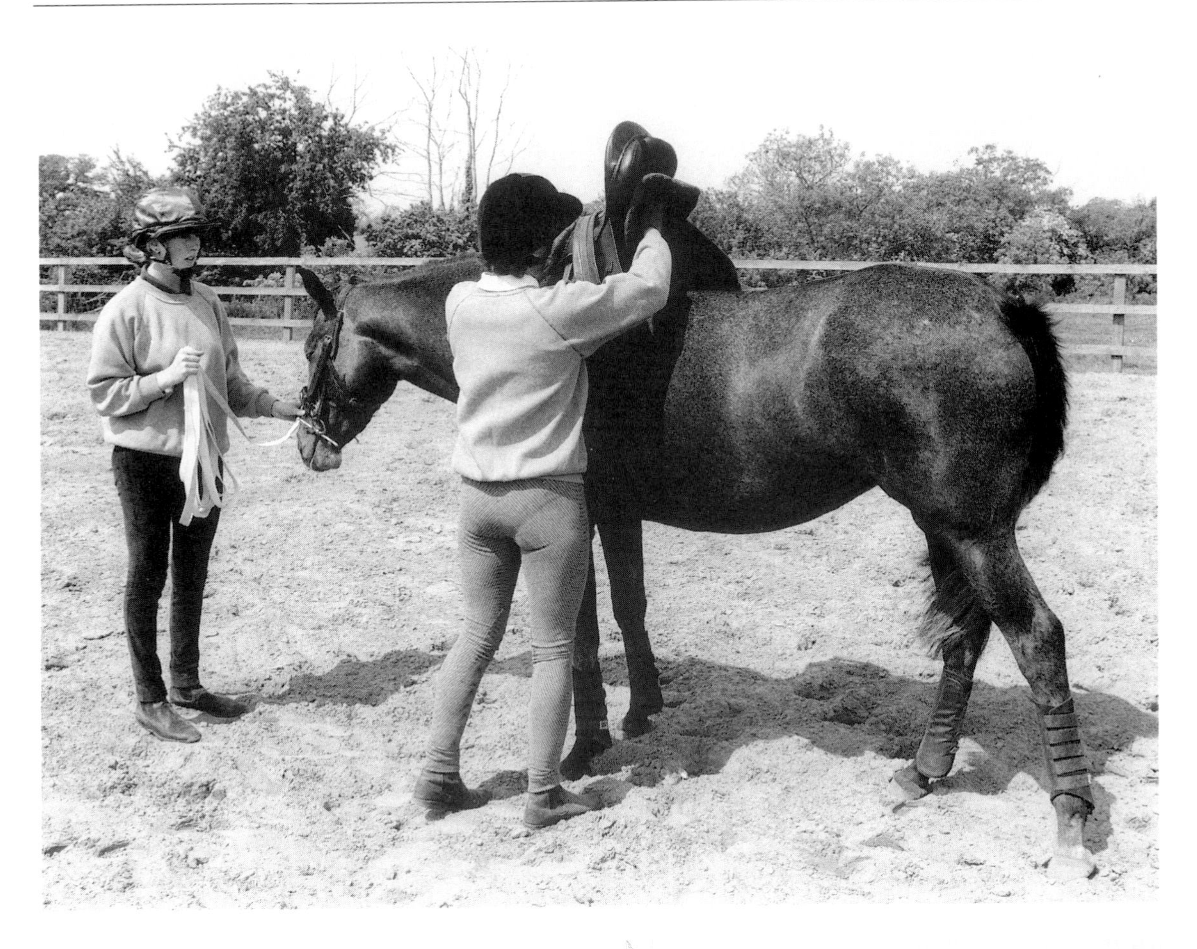

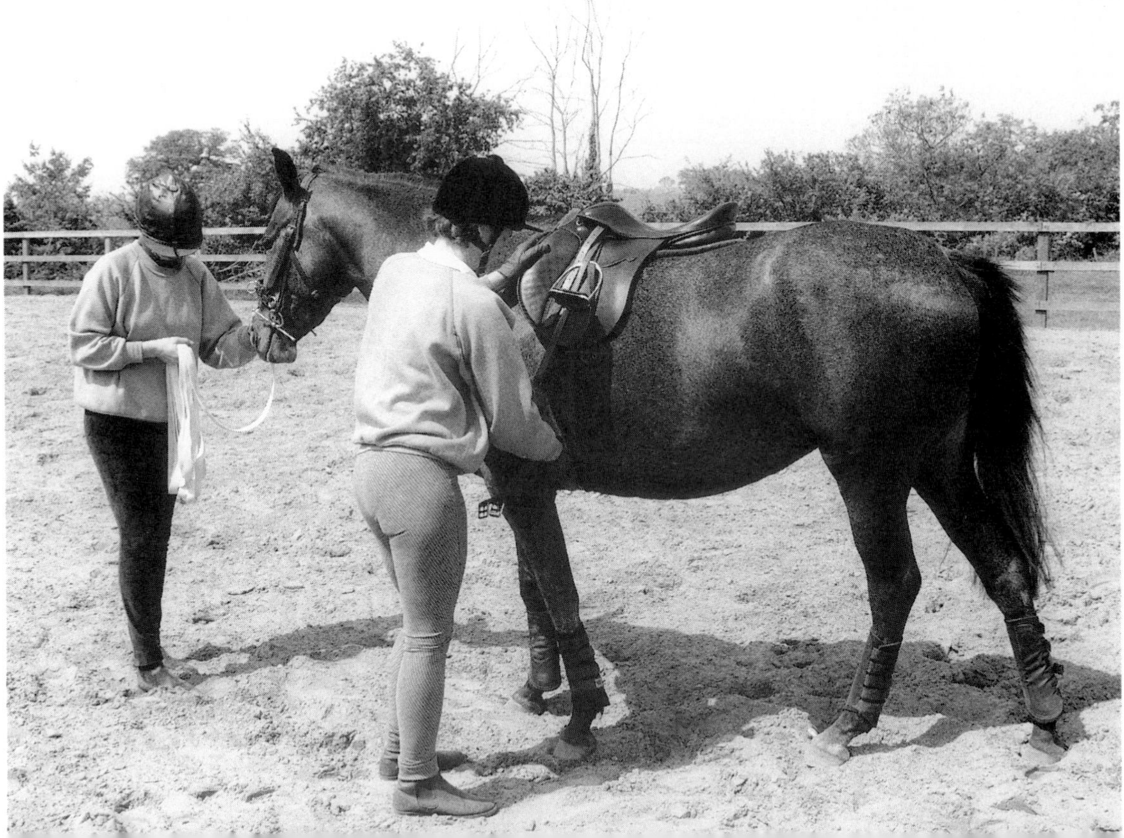

for anyone new to the activity to take a little time to learn how to do it safely, and how to use the equipment correctly. It is a good idea to practise on an older, more experienced horse at first, under the guidance of an experienced trainer.

Position

More than anything else, if you are a novice trainer, you need to learn how to position yourself in relation to the horse, in order to keep control. The idea is to guide the horse forward with your left hand and to drive him from behind – aided by the lungeing whip – with the right, if you are lungeing on the left rein, and vice versa if you are working on the right rein. In this way a triangle is formed between the horse's head, you and the horse's hindquarters **(fig. 16)**.

The novice trainer also needs to learn how to maintain a light, steady contact with the horse through the lungeing rein, and how to anticipate the horse's actions. This is achieved by adopting the correct stance: standing up straight yet relaxed, with feet slightly apart, and attentive to the horse at all times. From this position you will have every opportunity to control yourself and the horse, should he be startled or behave badly.

Holding the lunge line

There is also a safe way to hold the lunge line. Firstly, you should always wear gloves when lungeing, to prevent serious burns should the lunge rein be pulled through your hands. The excess rein (not used unless the horse is on full lunge) needs to be taken up by being looped in approximately 30 cm (1 ft) lengths. This is achieved by looping each loop on top of the last, so that the rein can be easily slipped in an emergency **(fig. 17)**.

The thumb secures the uppermost loop while the horse is being lunged. Under no circumstances should the lunge line be twisted round the hand or wrist in an attempt to gain a stronger hold over the horse, as this can result in burns, fingers being pulled off, or in your being dragged.

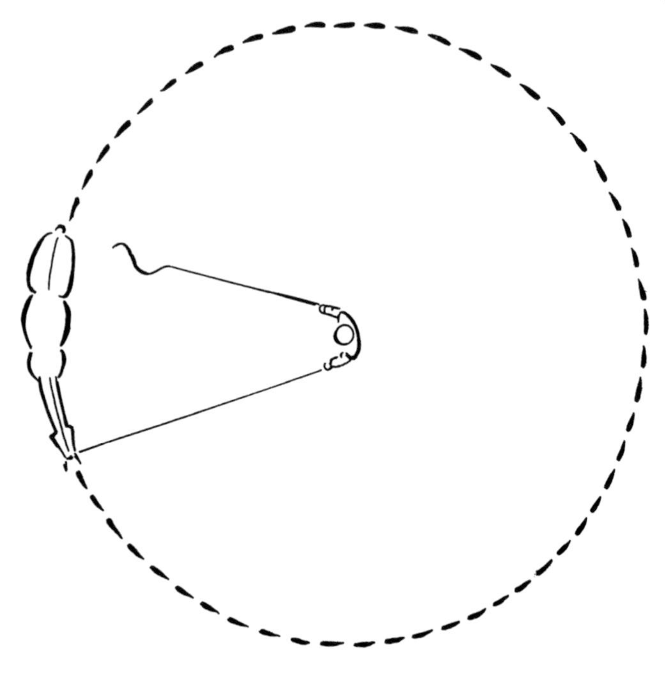

Fig. 16 The position of the trainer: a triangle is formed between the horse's head, the trainer and the horse's hindquarters

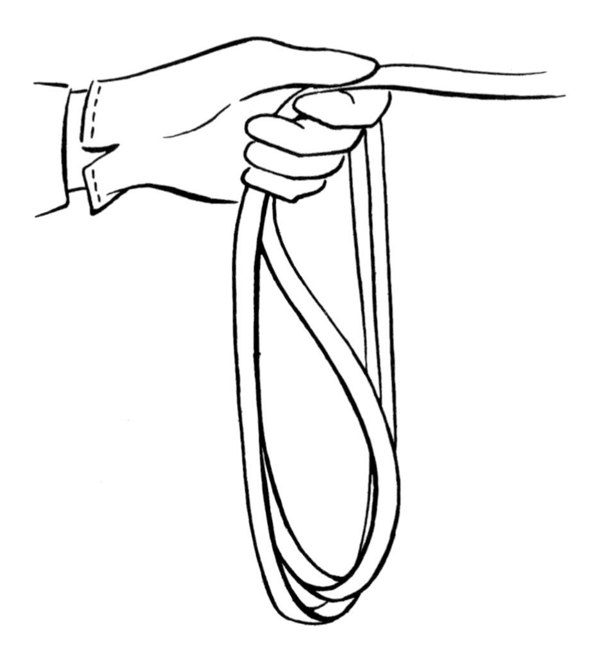

Fig. 17 The correct way to hold the lunge rein

Using the whip

The lunge whip is not a device used to punish the horse in any way, but is an aid to driving the horse forward. Lunge whips come in differing weights. You should acquire a whip that is well-balanced and light enough for you to be able to relax your hand while it is in use. The thong of the whip should be long enough to reach the horse **(fig. 18)**.

The thong of the whip rests on the floor, following the horse around the circle as he moves. The horse is made aware of its presence by a slight flick of the wrist, which ripples the thong. If the horse needs more encouragement, a sharper flick will make the thong give a small crack. Rarely does the horse need to be touched with the whip, but in such cases, where this is necessary the horse is simply 'touched' with the thong, and not struck with it.

The horse must learn to accept and respect the whip. He should not be made frightened of it, however, or he will learn to run from it, which defeats the object of lungeing. When approaching a horse while carrying the whip, it should be tucked under your arm, pointing backwards.

Once you are comfortable with these procedures, you should be able to lunge any horse at elementary level with confidence.

Preparation for the first lesson

On the day that lungeing is to commence, it is a good idea either to turn the horse out for an hour or two, or to loose school him first to allow him to 'let off steam'.

Prepare the horse for the lesson by putting on protective boots; these should always be used, as the young horse is often unco-ordinated and can knock himself easily. They also offer some support to the tendons, which are placed under greater strain when the horse is moving on a circle.

Roller or saddle the horse, and remove the stirrups. Put on the bridle, and either remove the reins, or twist them around each other under the horse's neck, and secure them by passing the throat lash through them. The use of a bit informs the

Fig. 18 The lunge whip that you use should be fairly light,with a thong that is long enough to reach the horse

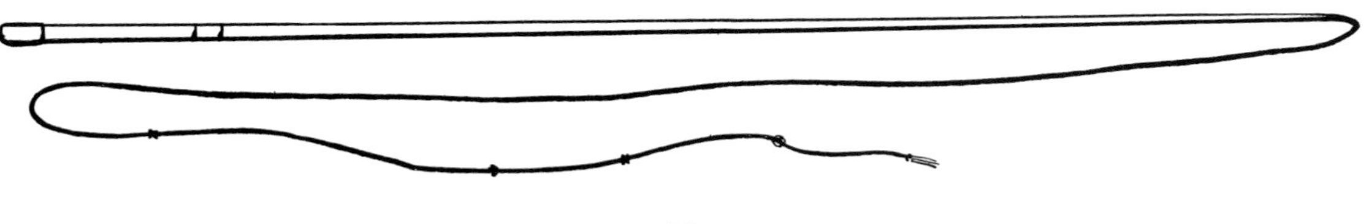

horse that a training session is about to commence, and establishes a routine and discipline.

Next, place the cavesson over the top of the snaffle bridle. Secure the noseband of the cavesson under the bridle cheek-pieces, above the bit, so that it does not interfere with the bit in any way. Side reins are not needed in the first few lessons, but come at a later stage (see pages 87–8).

Finally, attach the lunge line to the centre ring of the lungeing cavesson **(fig. 19)**. It is also a good idea to attach a lead rein to the bridle noseband. This will allow you to lead the horse safely to the school without putting pressure on his nose. Take up the whip, holding the thong along its length, and lead the horse to the working area.

Fig. 19 The horse prepared for his first lungeing session (*note:* the stirrups have been removed and the reins secured)

Using an assistant

It is possible to lunge a youngster for the first time entirely on your own, but it is safer and will be more successful if you engage the help of a willing assistant, at least for the first session.

Do not talk to your assistant once the session has begun, as the horse will be listening to your voice and will not understand that you are not making a request. Discuss what you wish your assistant to do before the lesson, and, if necessary, convey your wishes to him or her by nodding or similar 'sign language'.

Walk your horse to the outside track and ask him to stand. Ask your helper to hold the horse, and position yourself in the centre of the circle on which you will be working. Your helper is only there as a guide to the horse and should not try to control him too much. Ask your horse to walk on, starting on the left rein – most horses prefer the left rein, so it is easier to start in that direction **(45)**. Remember that it is always easier to ask the horse to comply with something that he finds fairly easy, before requesting anything more difficult and perhaps risking an unnecessary battle.

If your horse does not respond, ask again and signal to your assistant to move off at a slow pace. The horse will almost certainly follow. If he does not follow, do not ask your assistant to pull him forward. You yourself must drive him on by using your voice, stance and – if necessary – by flicking the lungeing whip towards his hocks.

Ask the horse to walk the outside track initially, and follow him yourself on a smaller rectangle, keeping about 1–1.5 m (4-5 ft) from his head, with your assistant walking on his off side. Once this is accomplished, start to describe a circle, and encourage the horse to follow at the length of the lunge line, while you gradually play it out.

At this stage, you will not be able to stand still in the centre of the circle, but should move along in time with the horse on a smaller circle **(fig. 20)**. with loose schooling, if you get in front of the horse's movement he will slow down, and if you get too far behind he will increase his pace. The aim here is to keep him moving steadily, so you must endeavour to maintain your position in relation to the movement.

Your assistant should guide the horse from the outside of the circle, while you control the movement from within. This method has the advantage of allowing direct contact between you and the horse, and affords the assistant a quick get-away should one be needed. Alternatively, he or she can simply fade away quietly when the time is right. This method causes few problems provided that the horse has been used to being led equally from both sides. The horse which has only been led from the near side may find being guided in this way a little confusing at first.

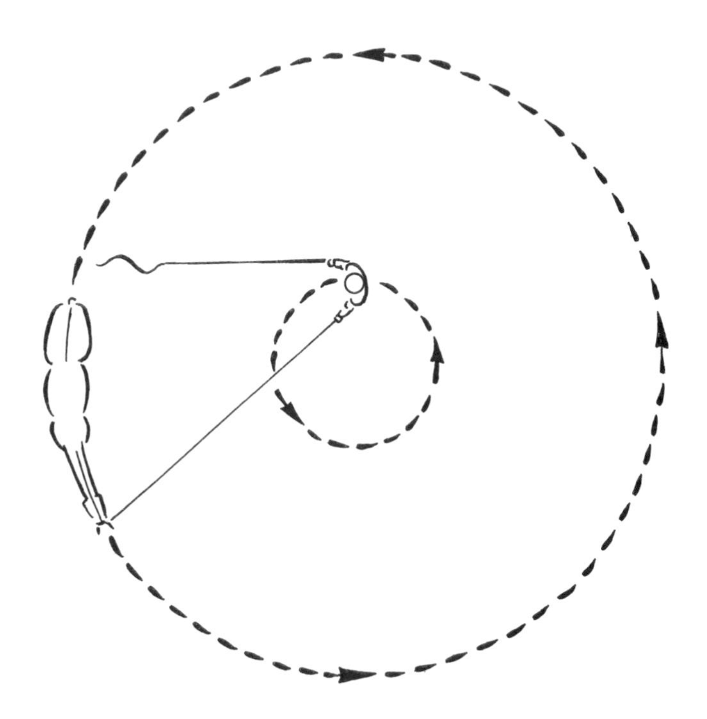

Fig. 20 You will need to move along in time with the horse, on a smaller circle

WILLOW

Lungeing without an assistant

If you have to lunge without the aid of an assistant, you can avoid difficult situations by using certain tactics.

Firstly, work at one end of the working area, where you can use at least two, or hopefully three, sides of the working area (depending on its size) to your advantage, so that they act as a natural guide.

Take your horse to the centre of your chosen working area, and encourage him to walk around you on the left rein. Do not place him on the outside track and expect him to walk happily around the school, as it is highly probable that he will simply turn in and come towards you.

Let out the lunge rein a little at a time, and place yourself level with the horse's hip. From here you are in an ideal position to drive him on, and he is less likely to spin round, which can be one of the major problems when lungeing on your own.

Be consistent and frequent with your verbal commands, and use the sides of the working area to guide the horse and to act as a speed break if he becomes too active. If the horse is rushing, for example, ask him to slow the pace when coming towards the end of the school so that he can see no way directly forward, rather than when leading him towards the middle of the school when all he can see is open space. Once he has stopped, reward him, and repeat the lesson until he responds to your command at any position in the school.

Always make much of the horse when he has complied with even the simplest of requests. This encourages him to *want* to understand and – just as importantly – to comply.

45 At first the horse is led around on the left rein by an assistant

Aims of the first few lessons

In the very first lesson, the horse has done enough when he has remained out on the track by himself – ideally on both reins, or with the helper still guiding him on the right rein.

In the next lesson, once the horse is walking freely round on the left rein, you can ask him to trot on **(46)**. The horse which has been loose schooled will almost certainly comply straight away. One which has not may need more encouragement by flicking the thong of the whip towards his quarters.

In order to keep the horse under control and in position, you will almost certainly need to move around a little, as he will not be perfectly balanced and may need to take a more oval track to keep himself steady. Although you should aim to stand in the centre as lungeing progresses, you must be prepared to allow the horse some movement from the circle until he is able to control himself more easily. Keep the lunge rein taut, and encourage the horse to take the full length given to him so that at no time does it become slack.

Once the horse has trotted a few circles, he will probably be ready to walk. Allow him to do so, but anticipate his action and ask for walk just as he is about to slow up himself. Reward him, and he will think that he has responded to your request, and will associate his action with the verbal command given.

When the horse is again walking on freely, ask him to stand. If necessary, slowly take in the rein and move more towards his front, so that you are no longer in a driving position. The horse will slow down naturally, and at this point you must be ready to keep him from turning in by pointing the lungeing whip directly at his shoulder if necessary. Be careful to do this slowly, however, and to hold the whip still.

When the horse is stationary, it is important that you approach him with the whip tucked behind your back, and that you make much of him. Do *not* call him towards you at any cost, as a horse which learns, or is encouraged, to turn in soon thinks he can do so whenever he wishes **(47)**.

46 The horse should be taught to stay out on the track when halted. He must never be encouraged to turn inward or to walk towards you, as this may become a tiresome habit

47 Once the horse walks freely around on the left rein, he is asked to trot on (*note:* the lunge rein is kept taut, but the trainer is not in a fixed position and is able to 'give' with the rein)

48 *(Above)* Cantering a young, unbalanced horse on a circle can cause injury. Here, however, the horse has decided to canter by himself. The trainer holds firm, but does not pull the horse's head around in an attempt to stop him. He is encouraged to slow down by voice

49 *(Left)* By the end of two weeks, the horse is moving freely forward in a nice, balanced rhythm

Provided that all has gone well, you can repeat the whole exercise to the right. Bear in mind, however, that most horses seem to find this rein more difficult, so you should be prepared to stop once the horse has walked the circle (or simply the outside track) a few times. Gauge how the horse is coping at this stage, and do not ask for more than he is capable of giving.

The next few lessons will simply be a repeat of the previous two. The horse is not asked to canter at this stage **(48)**. Your aim is simply to establish obedience and understanding, and not to undertake any serious schooling.

Within one to two weeks, the horse should have learned to remain on the circle by himself in walk and trot on both reins, and to halt and stand when requested without turning in. This should all be carried out calmly. Lungeing will continue for some time yet, but you should not aim to teach the horse much more at this stage. You will repeat what he has learned and aim to have him moving forward freely in a nice, balanced rhythm **(49)**, before embarking upon the next stage of long reining (see Chapter 6).

Working equally on both reins

As has already been mentioned, many horses seem to have greater difficulty establishing a good, steady rhythm on the right rein, but it is still essential to lunge them equally in both directions to ensure correct muscle development. Be sure to change the rein frequently to add variety and to help prevent boredom.

To change the rein, prepare for halt and ask with your voice and body position for halt at an appropriate moment. Make sure that the horse stands on the outside track and walk towards him, coiling up the rein as you go. Make much of the horse, and then lead him to the centre of the circle on which you are working. Change the lunge rein and whip into opposite hands and drive the horse off on the opposite rein to the one used before. Keep the lunge rein taut as you play it out by driving the horse forward and encouraging him to take up the slack.

When changing the rein, many horses will try to turn round and come in if they are not driven off strongly enough. It is crucial with the young horse that this is prevented from the start, as, once accomplished, it is a tiresome habit which is extremely hard to correct. You must therefore anticipate the horse's moves and be one step ahead at all times.

If by driving him off strongly the horse reacts by trotting off, allow him to do so, and simply wait until he settles into a steady rhythm before making a request to alter the pace.

Side reins

The use of side reins in the basic training of the young horse is often cause for debate among trainers. If side reins are misused, they can be very damaging to progress and can ruin the horse's mouth. If used correctly, however, they can certainly give good results. The problems develop when people who do not know how to fit side reins properly – or in fact why they are using them – do so regardless because they think that they are a necessary part of training.

There are various designs of side rein. Some are made of plain leather, while others have rubber or elastic inserts to provide an amount of 'give' in the contact **(fig. 21)**.

What you are actually trying to achieve by the use of side reins is a horse which is 'working through', or, as is often described, 'on the bit' (see pages 126–7). The aim is *not* to pull the horse's head into

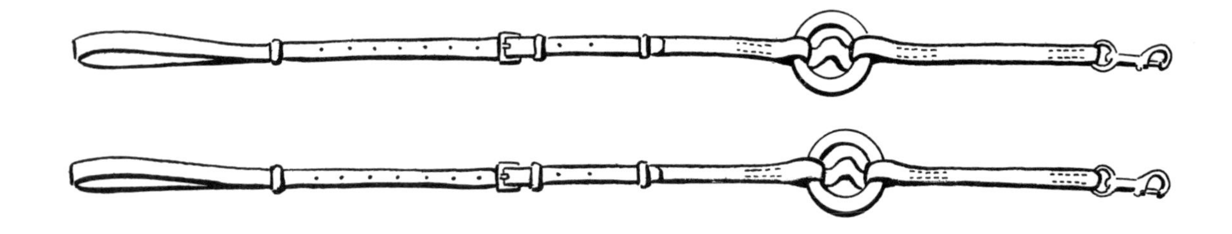

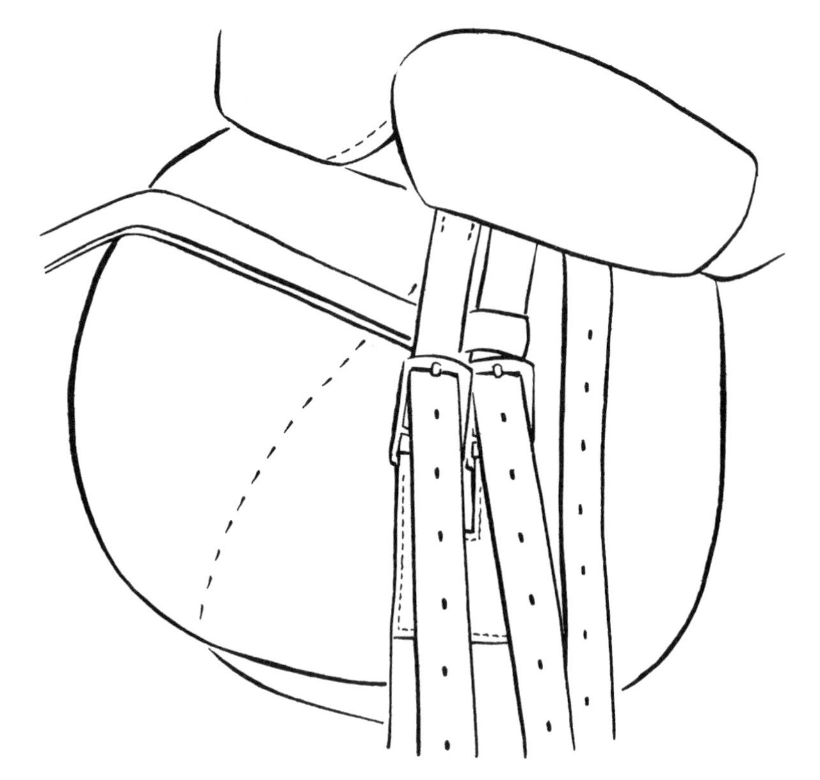

Fig 21 Side reins with rubber inserts are designed to afford a degree of 'give' in the contact

Fig. 22 Side reins are fitted above the girth buckles, so that they will not slip down when in use

position by fitting the reins tightly, but to encourage the horse to seek a contact with the bit through them, by engaging his hindquarters **(50)**.

If a horse shows signs of wanting to make contact with the bit, by working long and low, stretching his neck forward and down, then he is ready for the careful use of side reins. If he is not showing these signs and side reins are fitted, there is the risk that the horse will resist the contact, either by going behind the bit (where he falls behind the contact and 'over-bends'), or by coming above the bit (where he raises his head and hollows his back).

If the horse is ready for side reins, they should be attached loosely at first. Fix the reins to the saddle above the girth buckles, so that they will not slip down **(fig. 22)**, and clip them on to the 'D' rings of the

50 *(Right)* Side reins, if used, must be correctly fitted so that they do not pull the horse's head into an unnatural position

saddle. Allow the horse to work in for a few minutes before attaching the reins to the bit.

The reins should be of equal length and fairly long at first. Once the horse is accustomed to the feel of them, and is seeking contact, you can gradually shorten the reins over a period of sessions, until the required contact – which will help to develop a good outline – is achieved **(51)**. The idea behind this procedure is that the horse will not learn to fear the contact, because he has established it himself.

Establishing a routine, not a programme

By following the above procedure, a routine will emerge which suits each horse, but you should not aim for a set 'programme', when lungeing. A working routine is always beneficial, as the horse anticipates his lessons and his mind becomes conditioned to working at the times set by you – once in the morning and once in the afternoon, for example. This could be broken up by turning the horse

51 The side reins should be shortened gradually until a good outline is established

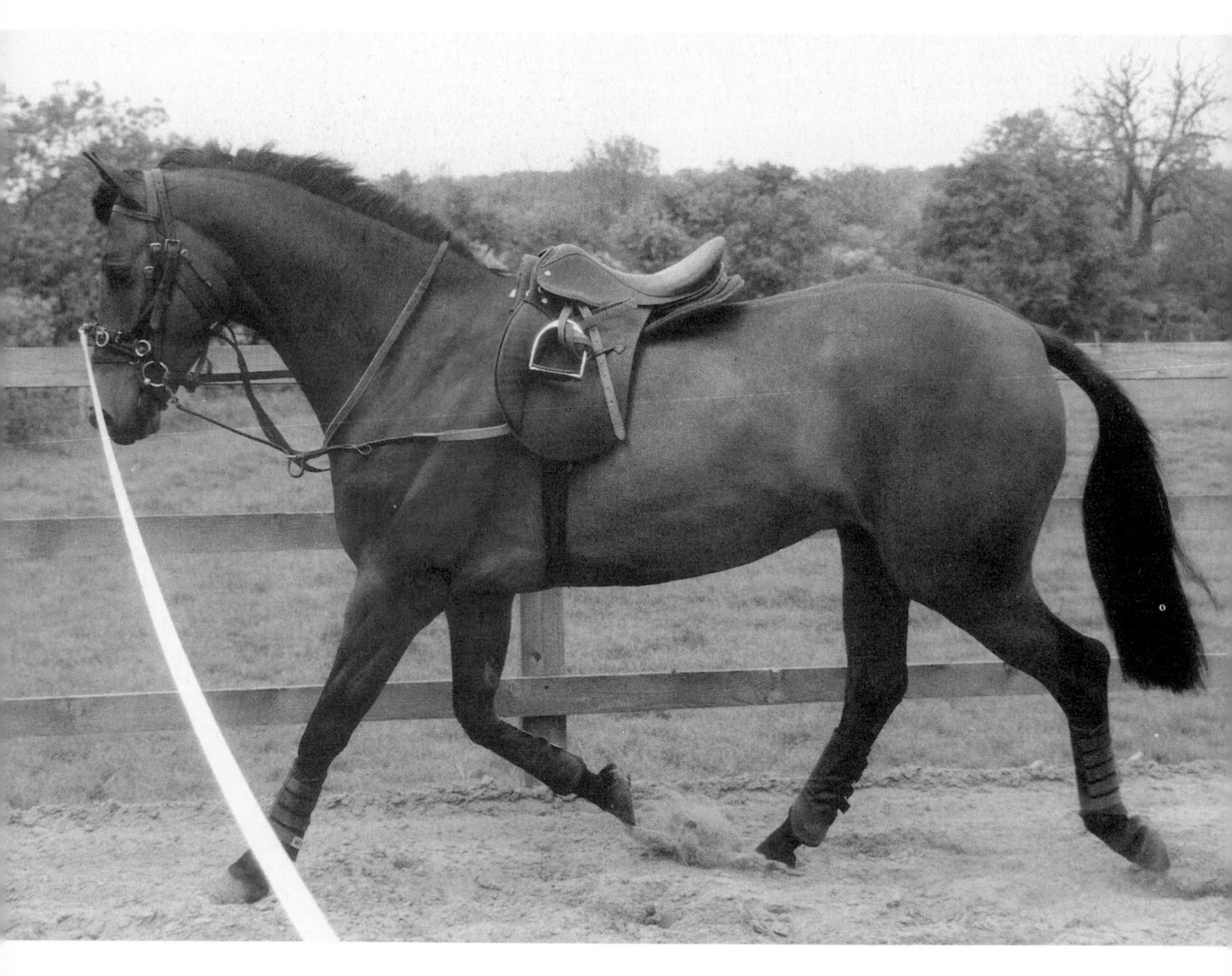

KEEPING THE LESSON SHORT

- The very first lesson with side reins must be a very short one. If the aims previously described have not been achieved, you should put the horse away and bring him out for another short session later in the day. Two ten-minute sessions are of greater benefit than one twenty-minute one.
- The duration of sessions can be increased as the days pass, but be prepared to finish a session if the horse responds quickly to requests. Treating each horse individually is the only way to ensure that you are working at the right pace for each horse. As a guide, however, you might aim to start with two ten-minute sessions on the first day, increasing to two twenty-minute sessions by the end of two weeks.
- If all has gone well, long reining can then commence (see Chapter 6).

out or walking him out, or by loose schooling, which may still continue as a form of exercise and enjoyment.

Following a set programme within the lesson, however, is not a good idea. Although at the beginning of the young horse's training you may always ask him to lead off in walk, you should not always follow this with the same request. Sometimes you should ask him to halt and change the rein, and at other times ask him to trot on, walk again, then perhaps trot again. If he knows that after walking he will be asked to trot, then walk and halt, always in the same sequence, he will begin to anticipate the movements and lose concentration. *Variation* is the key to keeping the horse attentive.

KEY POINTS

- Loose schooling can be most enjoyable for both horse and trainer.
- Be certain of the words that you intend to use for each pace and for rewarding the horse, and stick to them throughout his training.
- Lungeing horses is a skill within the scope of anyone dedicated to training youngsters, provided that the time is taken to learn the correct techniques.
- More than anything else, the novice trainer needs to learn how to position him or herself in relation to the horse, in order to keep control.
- The lunge whip is not a device used to punish the horse in any way, but is an aid to driving him forward.
- It is possible to lunge a youngster for the first time entirely on your own, but it is safer and will be more successful if you can engage the help of an assistant, at least for the first session.
- If you have to lunge without the aid of an assistant, you can avoid difficult situations by using certain tactics.
- Always make much of the horse when he has complied with even the simplest of requests.
- The aim in the first few weeks is for the horse to remain on the circle by himself in walk and trot on both reins, and to halt and stand when requested without turning in. This should all be carried out calmly.
- It is essential that the horse works equally on both reins to ensure correct muscle development.
- Two ten-minute sessions are of greater benefit than one twenty-minute session.
- Establish a working routine, but avoid programming – variation is the key to keeping the horse attentive.

6

LONG REINING

A training method in its own right

Long reining is less widely used in the preparation of youngsters than lungeing, and yet the English method is particularly suitable for the younger horse, when the aim is for him to achieve a longer outline. Many people seem to be dissuaded from long reining because they feel that it is a difficult skill to learn.

This may indeed be true for the continental methods, where long reining is used for highly advanced, collected schooling work. In the training of the young horse, however, the long reins are an excellent medium through which basic exercises can be taught, which – once the horse is backed – will be reinforced by the rider.

Long reins afford the trainer the benefit of actually seeing, as well as feeling, how the horse is performing. Although long reining of the young horse is used as a bridge between lungeing and backing, it is therefore also a useful training method in its own right.

A great rapport can be established between horse and trainer, which is one of the reasons why the activity is often continued throughout a horse's career. In fact, a good trainer can accomplish the same degree of training with long reins as under saddle. Some trainers are so proficient, and have such an excellent rapport with their equine pupils, that they are capable of achieving Grand Prix dressage movements with their actions being apparent only to the most experienced eye.

There are four methods which can be used to long rein the horse through various stages in his life: the Danish, French and Viennese methods and the English method, which, being best-suited to the training of youngsters, is the method we will follow.

THE OBJECTIVES OF LONG REINING

- Long reining builds up the young horse's confidence and trust.
- It reinforces obedience.
- It teaches the horse more 'intimate' manners.
- It builds up the muscles and increases suppleness.
- It gives the young horse a good mouth before he is ridden.

Extending training on the lunge

Long reining follows on nicely from lungeing. You can still work the horse on a circle, and, because you will have greater control, you can ask for a degree of 'lightness' and self-carriage. Long reining has the advantage over lungeing in that you can also work the horse on curves, serpentines, figure-of-eights and straight lines.

Equipment

There is no need to acquire special equipment for the basic training that a young horse will receive on long reins. If the horse has been lunged as described in Chapter 5, you will have all the equipment that you need, excepting an extra lunge rein. However, the equipment is fitted and used in a different way.

Firstly, the two reins should not be shorter than 7.5 m (25 ft) each in length. The width is an important consideration, because, if you will be long reining through a roller, the reins need to be thin enough to slide easily through the rings. Needless to say, they should of course still be very strong (canvas or nylon are generally used). Each rein must be separate, with a knot tied in the end to prevent it from slipping through your hands.

If you use a roller, this should be padded. If the roller is to be used throughout, it will also need two sets of rings on either side: one set for mouthing the horse, and the other for further work lower down.

Many people also use a whip when long reining. A good, lightweight and fairly long schooling whip is quite suitable, although the lungeing whip can also be used. Whether or not you use a whip will depend on how well the horse responded to your body position when loose schooling and lungeing – some people tend not to use one at all.

The horse's ordinary snaffle bridle should be used, but for the first few sessions a lungeing cavesson will need to be worn as well.

It is perfectly acceptable to long rein using an ordinary saddle. In this case, the long reins pass through the stirrups, which, if in the longer position, are secured underneath the horse's belly by a plain leather strap which sits on top of the girth **(fig. 23)**. In fact, once the horse has been mouthed (see page 97), it is more desirable to use a saddle, as the stirrup height can be adjusted to accommodate different levels of training as and when necessary.

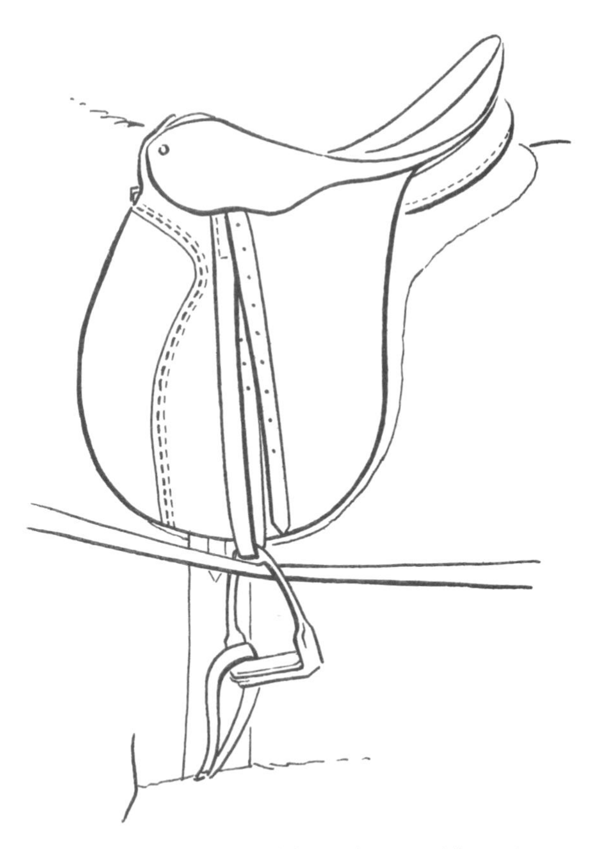

Fig 23 If you are long reining using a saddle and longer-length stirrups, the stirrups should be secured by a plain leather strap, which passes under the horse's belly and sits on top of the girth

Preparing for the first session

As with lungeing, the surface of the working area needs to be considered. You must ensure that it is not slippery, especially if it has already been used extensively for lungeing. If the surface does become a little wet, a mixture of sand and wood-chippings can be put down (this may need to be covered with polythene after schooling to stop it from becoming saturated should it rain, and some large boulders around the edge will secure the polythene if it becomes windy).

Before you can commence work on long reins, the horse needs to be prepared for his sessions. In your favour, you already have a horse which is used to wearing the equipment and which trusts and obeys you. Your horse also knows your voice commands and is familiar with the working area.

The horse now needs to become used to the aids which you will use. These are: the reins themselves, the whip, your position and your voice. Although the horse has been accustomed to these when lungeing, you are now going to ask him to accept them being used in another way.

Getting used to the reins

Tack up the horse as for lungeing, with one rein attached to the middle ring of the cavesson, and lead him into the working area. Give him a period of lungeing as normal.

For the next stage, it is very useful if you can again employ the assistance of a willing helper to help you to put the reins in position safely, but it is possible to do this on your own if necessary. If an assistant is not available, the following procedure should be carried out in a stable.

Ask the horse to stand, and arm yourself with the second rein. Lay this (unattached) across the horse's back and gently droop it around his back and quarters a little. Gradually allow the loose end to hang down over the tail and play around the horse's hocks. He may kick back a little when he feels this but will soon come to accept it.

Next, run the second rein through the ring on the right of the roller, or through the right stirrup, and attach it to the right-hand side ring of the lungeing cavesson. Then place this rein over the horse's quarters, and position yourself at the horse's hip – the left rein coming directly from the cavesson, the right rein coming through the roller ring or stirrup, over the quarters to you on the horse's left side.

At this initial stage, it is important to have the inside rein coming directly to you from the cavesson, not through the roller ring or stirrup **(52)**. This is because – in the event of your needing to stop the horse quickly – you can do so by letting loose the outside rein and quickly looping up the inside rein so that you are at his head in moments with a secure hold. If the horse were to pull back for any reason with the inside rein through the stirrup, it would act as a lever, pulling the horse away from you further. In order to get hold of the horse's head you would have to let go of the rein – and him – in which time he could turn on his heels and be off round the working area with reins flying – an extremely dangerous situation.

Similarly, you *should* anchor the outside rein through the stirrup or ring, to prevent it from dropping down lower than the horse's hocks. This would annoy him, and create the risk of him possibly being caught up in it in some way if he flicked his legs backwards.

Once you have both reins attached, you can begin to use them. If you have been working in the stable up to this point, you

52 When first long reining, the inside rein comes directly to the trainer from the cavesson. The outside rein, which is anchored through the roller ring or stirrup, rests above the horse's hocks

should now bring the horse to the working area and repeat the process here before continuing. Holding the inside rein in your left hand, flick the right rein around the horse's quarters and allow it to rest above his hocks. Ask the horse to walk on and follow him, guiding with the inside rein, driving with the outside rein and keeping your position level with his hip.

Having already been accustomed to the outside rein around his hocks, the horse is unlikely to do very much other than walk on quietly. If he does react to the pressure of the rein, it is only likely to be by kicking back a couple of times, or by rushing forward for a few paces. He will soon settle, and you should continue to walk around the track with him for a few circuits on fairly short reins. After this, ask him to halt by moving towards his shoulder while applying slight pressure on both reins, and then gather up the reins.

At first, gathering up long reins can be a bit of a handful, but there is an easy procedure. Hold both reins in one hand and slide the other hand up both reins, towards the horse's head, shortening them as you go. Make sure that the outside rein is not underneath the horse's tail.

To teach the horse to move off, you firstly need to consider his temperament. Some horses are by nature more flighty than others, and will only need to be told to walk on, with a slight relaxation on the rein. Others may need to see the whip, accompanied by the voice command and relaxation of the rein, before they get the idea.

To change the rein in this first session, simply halt the horse, reverse the rein that is free and the rein that is through the roller ring or stirrup, and turn the horse around. Then proceed as before, walking a few circuits in the opposite direction. Ask the horse for halt and gather up the reins again.

This is all that needs to be done in preparation for working the horse in long reins properly, although you may need to repeat the exercise again in the next session.

To detach the outside rein, always unclip it from the cavesson or bit *before* running it back through the roller ring or stirrup. To attach the outside rein, always run it through the stirrup or roller ring *before* clipping it to the cavesson or bit.

How to long rein

In the next few long-reining sessions, you will work with the reins in the same way, practising walking and trotting on both reins, still with the reins attached to the cavesson and the inside rein coming directly to you.

As it is tiresome to keep stopping to change the rein, the next lesson involves changing the rein while in motion. This is achieved by gradually walking a large 'S' bend **(fig. 24)**. The inside hand guides the horse, indicating the direction in which you wish him to go, and the outside hand prevents his quarters from swinging out. Do not pull on the inside rein to alter the bend, but work on 'giving' the outside rein, and therefore keeping as light a contact as possible. As you come to the middle of the 'S', you will in fact be

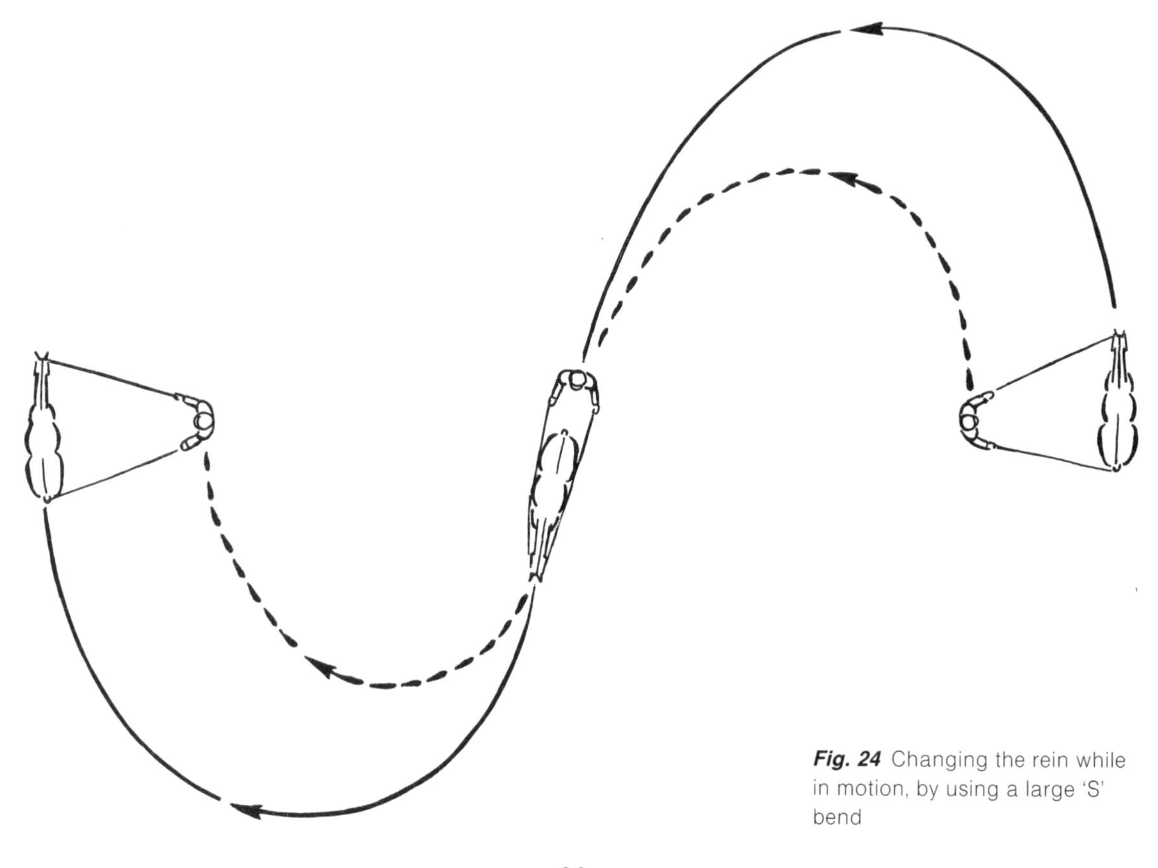

Fig. 24 Changing the rein while in motion, by using a large 'S' bend

walking behind the horse for a few paces, before altering your leading and driving hands.

If the horse becomes at all unsettled while doing this, you can use an intermediate stage. Guide the horse forward along the first section of the 'S' and, when you are immediately behind him, at the point at which you are about to alter guiding and driving hands, ask for halt. Slowly alter your hands and position so that you are on the opposite rein, and then ask your horse to walk on once more. Once you have established the change of rein, you can go on to the next stage: mouthing the horse.

Mouthing

Mouthing teaches the horse the action of the bit, and I believe that this is best done through the long reins.

Some trainers prefer to start mouthing the horse by using side reins on the lunge before backing. I feel, however, that, as the youngster at this stage is not yet developed or balanced, he cannot establish the level of impulsion required to take up the correct contact with the bit through the side reins. In consequence, you risk the horse trying to evade the bit, either by putting his head low (overbending) in order to ease the contact, or by bringing his head up too high. Alternatively, he may simply set himself against the reins by pulling or leaning.

Through the long reins, you can feel the exact extent of contact that you have with the horse's mouth, and can therefore mouth him more sympathetically, encouraging him to take up the light, even contact that is desired **(53)** and **(54)**. The aim of any good long-rein handler is to develop a steady hand, which maintains a light contact, through which kind but definite requests are given.

As soon as the horse is going freely forward from the cavesson and has learned to change the rein, you can attach the long reins directly to the bit rings, in order for the horse to be mouthed and further work to commence.

Once the reins are coming to you directly from the bit, you must ensure that you do not establish a 'dead' contact on the mouth, nor pull back on the reins **(55)**. At this stage you want the horse to be moving forward in a nice free-and-easy rhythm, so, although you need to take up any slack in the reins, you must not make the horse feel restricted in any way **(56)**.

The use of exercises while long reining

In order to perform exercises of real benefit, you need to be sure of working the reins in rhythm with the horse. To do this, observe the horse's legs, and, by positioning yourself slightly behind the horse's inside hip, encourage forward movement when horse's inside leg is not in contact with the ground. If carried, the whip can also be used occasionally to encourage impulsion, but, in the main, this is carried facing backwards. Sometimes you will need to work up fairly close to the horse, while at other times you can work further away, depending on the exercise being performed. The optimum distance for most basic work is about 3 m (10 ft) from the horse.

Once you have taught the horse to accept the long reins, you can move on to further his mental and physical education. This includes:

- developing his muscles and tendons
- working on him to increase his suppleness
- asking him to obey your requests to a finer degree

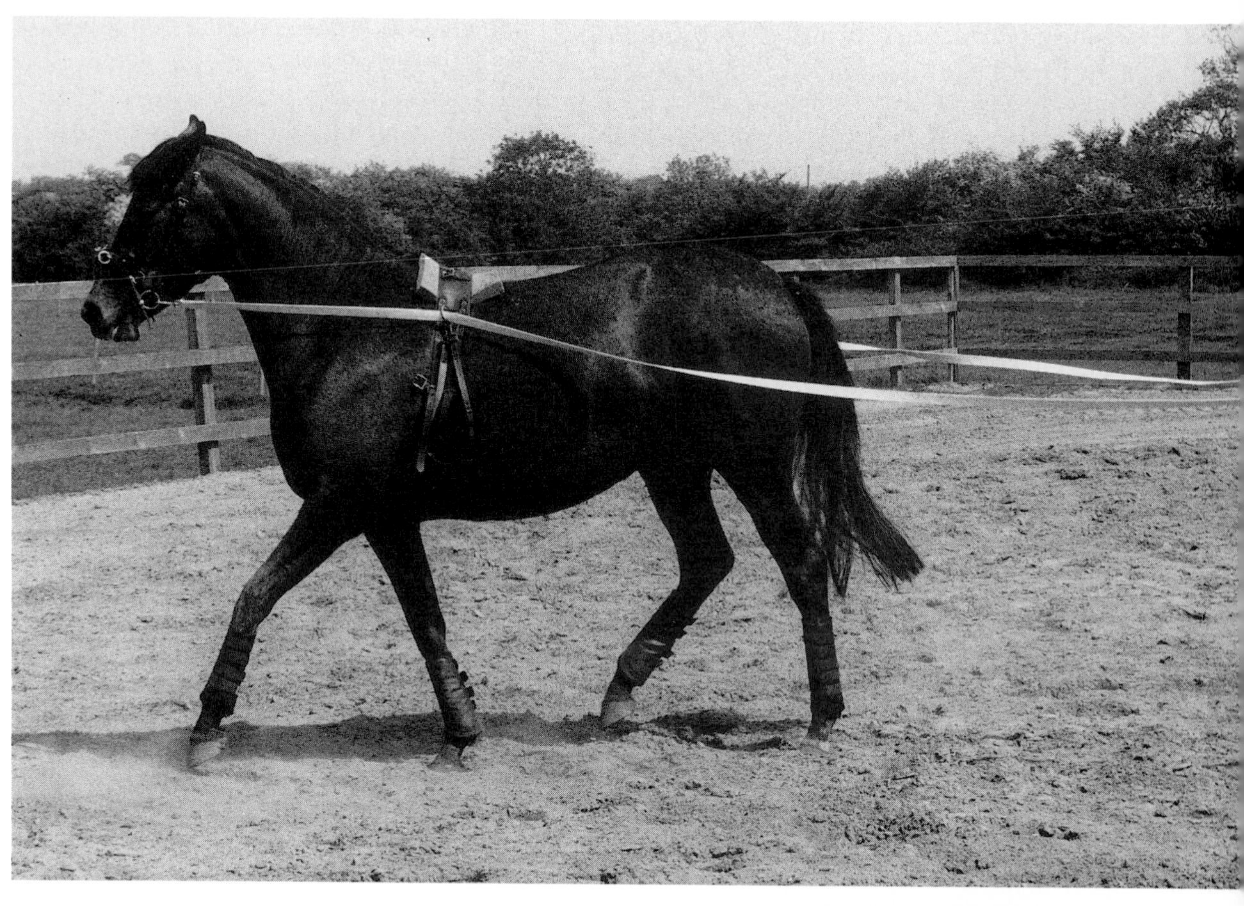

You will in fact be moving up a gear, and your horse may find the work more tiring than usual. You need to be aware of this and stop frequently, working a little at a time and being satisfied with small accomplishments.

The early exercises that a horse needs to learn are to move off calmly, walk and trot on actively, halt squarely, to change the rein and to accept the bit in a relaxed manner. You can make sure that this has been accomplished by working the horse on the circle, in straight lines and on curves, or in fact in any direction you choose. The most important consideration in whether the horse has learned his early exercises is that he complies with our requests when asked, and does not resist in any way.

This is all that is necessary for you to go on and back the horse with confidence and understanding. Any further training that you wish to do in long reins comes under the heading of advanced work, and is explained further in Chapter 9.

Confidence-building

During the horse's long-reining period before backing, he can be encouraged to have confidence in going to places on his own **(57)**. Once he is under total control, you can long rein him away from the working area: around the yard or farm, through the fields and along quiet lanes, experiencing new and varied terrain **(fig. 25)**. He will meet all sorts of new things, see houses, cars, dogs and trees and should be encouraged to go boldly past every-

53 Mouthing the horse on long reins (*note:* the horse is resisting at first, but is not being restricted)

54 The horse is beginning to accept the contact and to lower his head

Fig. 25 *(Above)* Long reining away from the working area encourages the horse to have confidence when meeting new objects and going to places on his own

55 *(Top left)* Long reining from the bit, through the stirrups and directly into the trainer's hands

56 *(Left)* A free forward movement is important – so if the horse goes, you must go with him, trying your best to use your voice and position to steady him

thing new that he encounters. He should also be taught to stand and wait until given the instruction to move off, when you open gates or meet traffic along narrow lanes.

Today, most young horses accept traffic from a very early age. Some horses can be apprehensive, however, and it is a good idea to get an assistant to drive a car gently past or up to a young horse in a yard or his own surroundings, before submitting him to traffic for the first time in new and frightening conditions, away from the safety of his own home.

As you will need to have total control from the moment you leave the stable to the moment you return, it is sensible to teach the horse to drive straight out of the stable and straight back in again **(figs. 26 and 27)**. Some horses will try to rush when doing this, while others may be a little more apprehensive, although most simply

Fig. 26 *(Top right)* When long reining away from the working area, you will need complete control throughout, so you should teach the horse to drive straight out of the stable

Fig. 27 *(Bottom right)* And straight back in again

57 *(Below)* The horse is keen to get going and takes no notice of large obstacles to which he has become accustomed

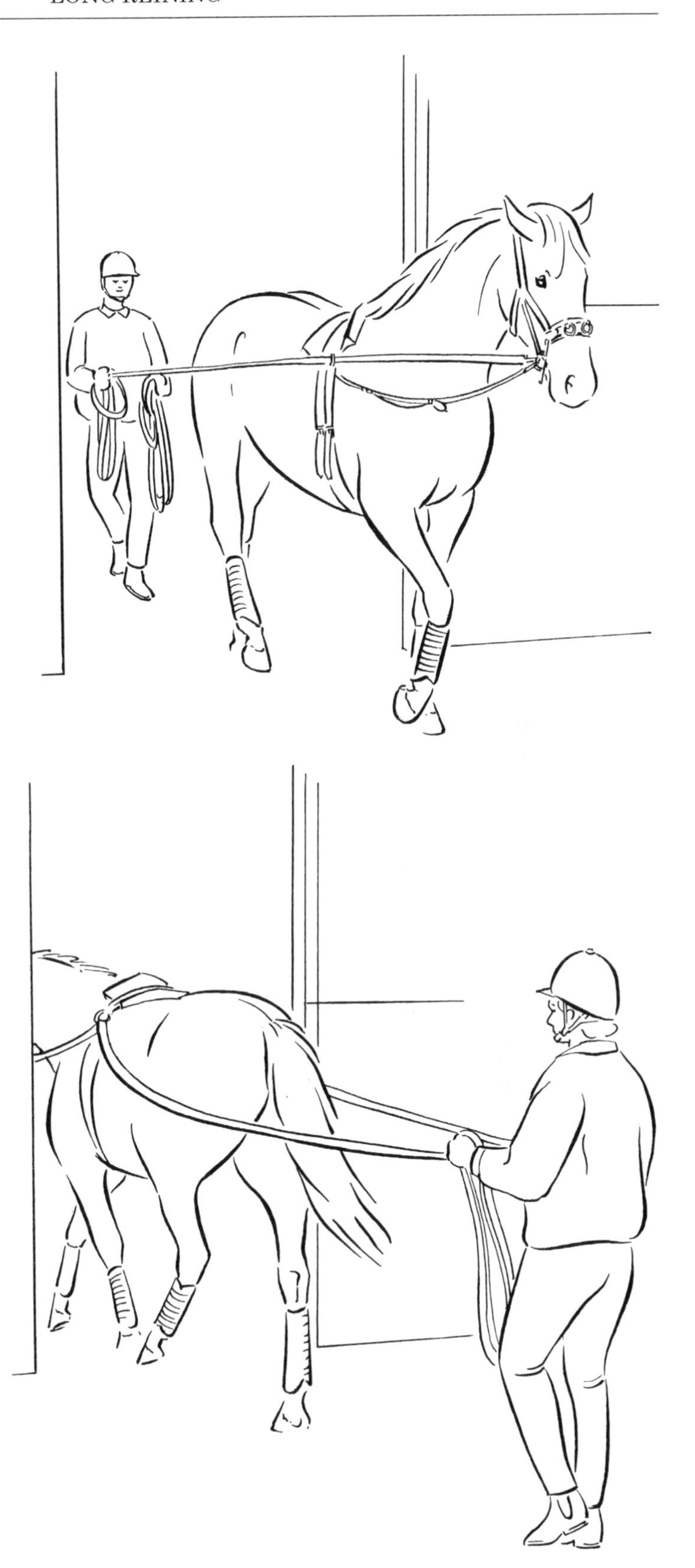

walk out or in quite calmly as required. It is all a question of confidence, and you should encourage the horse with your voice.

Giving the horse this sort of experience will be invaluable when it comes to hacking out for the first few times, especially if there is not a sensible lead horse available.

Boredom

You also need to ensure that the horse does not become bored or stale, so reward him often for compliance with your requests, and continue the principle of varying his work as much as possible. As he will be finding the work more demanding, you should ensure that he has plenty of freedom so that you are not risking his mental state. You can lead him out to graze if he is stabled, turn him out with other youngsters and take him for quiet walks along country lanes. Your horse will be more confident and happy as a result, because he will always be interested in any work that he is doing.

KEY POINTS

- Many people seem to be dissuaded from long reining because they feel that it is a difficult skill to learn, but this is not the case.
- In the training of the young horse, long reins are an excellent medium through which basic exercises can be taught.
- A proficient trainer can accomplish the same degree of training with long reins as under saddle.
- Long reining has the advantage over lungeing in that you can also work the horse on curves, serpentines, figure-of-eights and straight lines.
- In the initial stages of long reining, it is important to have the inside rein coming directly to the hand from the cavesson, not through the roller ring or stirrup.
- Mouthing is the procedure by which the horse is taught the action of the bit.
- Once you have taught the horse to accept long reins, you can move on to further mental and physical education.
- The prevention of boredom means that the horse will be more confident and happy, because he will always be interested in any work that he is doing.

7
BACKING

When is a horse ready to be backed?

Backing is the act of mounting for the first time, but no riding of the horse is involved. Backing is carried out when the horse is obedient to the trainer on the lunge and in long reins – on average, about two months after the starting process has begun.

Although the horse will now be physically stronger than before his training sessions, having a rider up on his back will entail the use of muscles which have not been required before. For this reason, backing must be done slowly and gently. Even the quietest, most obedient horse on the lunge can become apprehensive when first mounted, and so you must work through gradually, allowing him to become accustomed to a person's weight and movement on his back.

It is at this stage that you will need to exercise extreme patience, and to be satisfied with small accomplishments at first. If you rush, especially on the first day, you will run the risk of making the horse worried and anxious, which will cause problems when it comes to riding away.

PREPARATION TIPS FOR BACKING

- You can ensure that the day of backing goes smoothly in several ways.
- In order to accustom the horse to seeing someone higher than himself behind his eyes, lead him to a mounting block each day before or after training sessions and simply stand up on the block until he takes no notice. This should be done from both sides.
- Familiarize the horse with the noise of the saddle by slapping it and rocking it back and forth (58).
- Accustom him to pressure in the stirrups by pushing down in them with your arms, and to the feel of the rider's legs by lungeing with the stirrups down.

Who should back him?

The question of who should back the horse is often debated. Some trainers feel that the person who has trained the horse up until this point should not be the first to mount, as he or she should be holding the horse, and acting as a calming influence by using familiar words. Others hold with the view that a lightweight rider should always be the first to mount.

In my view, it seems sensible that the

first person to mount should be the one who has no qualms in doing so. Few well-trained horses 'put up a show', but some people cannot help being apprehensive – especially if they have never backed a horse before – and this will be transmitted to the horse.

It is dangerous to attempt to back a horse for the first time on your own, and so an assistant *must* be on hand at this stage. The duties of the assistant and person mounting are clearly defined. The assistant is responsible for managing the horse, and the person who is backing concentrates on staying in place. It is impossible for the person mounting to try to control the horse in any way, and so both people must have complete trust in one another's abilities to carry out the tasks competently.

Backing procedure

Some trainers back horses in their stables, because they feel that the confined space prevents any thought in the horse's mind of trying to get free. I prefer not to do this, as – should the horse do anything silly – the confined space can actually make the situation worse. The assistant could be squashed against the wall, and the person mounting could be squashed on the ceiling!

Some trainers also use a mounting block to mount for the first time. Again, I prefer not to do this, as the horse can easily bang against it or the assistant trip over it if the horse suddenly lurches away. Instead, I would advise that you take the horse to his normal working area, which he already

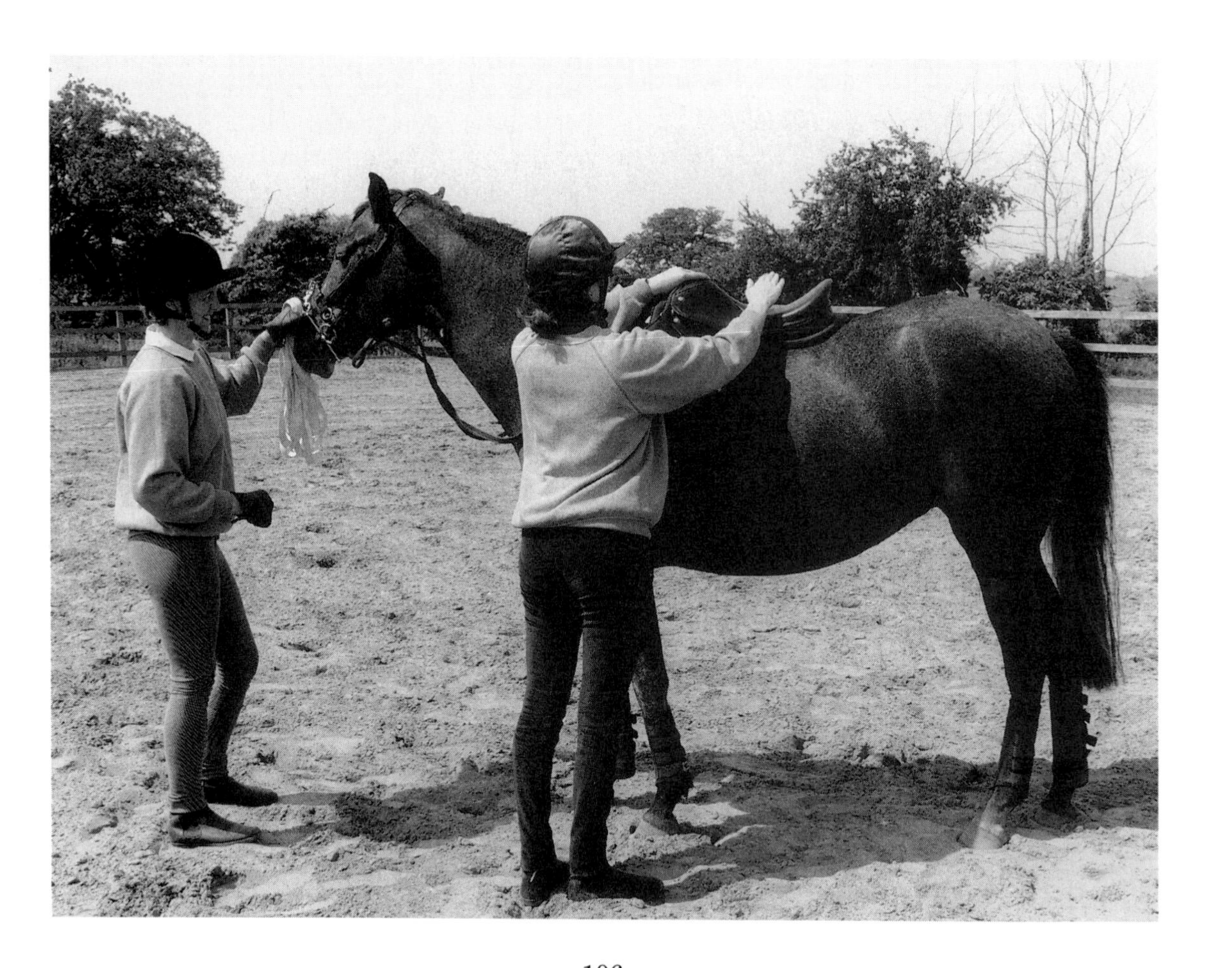

associates with obedience to training requests.

Remove the stirrups for the first session, tack up the horse for lungeing, and walk him to the working area. You should then lunge him on both reins as normal.

Leaning over the withers

Bring the horse into the middle of the school, and halt him squarely. Gather up the lunge line and take hold of the horse, talking in a soothing manner, while the person who is going to mount (who from now on we will call the rider) puts pressure on the saddle with his or her arms.

Still holding the horse by the lunge line, face the horse's shoulder and smoothly give the rider a leg up until he or she is lying over the saddle **(59** and **60)**. The rider then strokes the horse and talks to him constantly, while you offer him a carrot or a few nuts **(61)**. The rider then slips back down to the floor, makes much of the horse and the process is repeated again a few times. In most cases, the horse is so pleased to be getting a treat that he takes very little notice of the whole event.

It will depend on each individual horse whether any more can be done at this stage. If the horse seems to accept the rider, he or she can then move to the horse's right side and repeat the procedure. If the horse seems a little nervous, it would be wiser to put him away and have another session later in the day.

There is no benefit in rushing at this stage, and it is wise to allow the horse to dictate the pace. The tactful trainer is perceptive to the horse's state of mind, and

58 *(Left)* Before backing, the horse is accustomed to the noise of the saddle by slapping it and rocking it back and forth

59 *(Right)* The assistant smoothly gives the rider a leg up

60 She lies over the saddle at first

61 *(Left)* The rider then strokes and talks to the horse

62 *(Right)* Having accepted the rider over his back, the horse is walked on (*note:* the trainer walks backwards so that she can see exactly what is happening)

chooses the most appropriate course of action accordingly.

Staying up

The rate at which you proceed from here will depend on the individual horse, but it is wise to spend a few days repeating previous lessons just to make sure that the horse totally accepts what is happening, before moving on. You should not aim to do things so quickly that the horse is given no time to think, as, in such cases, the horse tends to rebel later on.

Once the horse has accepted the rider lying over his back, you can walk him around with the rider in this position **(62)**. Horses very rarely react to having weight on their backs while standing still, and, if there is to be any reaction, it is most likely to come – if at all – when he is moved. When first moving off with the rider lying over the horse's back, you must therefore be prepared for a reaction. If it comes, halt the horse immediately, and repeat the process once more, until he is walking around calmly.

Next, the rider slips his or her right leg over the saddle and gently sits in place, still leaning forward so as not to startle the horse **(63)**. Gradually the rider sits up and pats the horse, offering soothing words the whole time. Again, this should be repeated several times. The rider then dismounts with the same caution, and the stirrups are put back in place.

The next lesson will see the rider mounted and being led. He or she is given a leg up in the same way, and, once mounted, puts both feet into the stirrups **(64)**. As soon as the rider is in place, lead the horse off on to the track. Again, you must both be ready in case the horse gives any reaction, although, if this is done smoothly, there are unlikely to be any

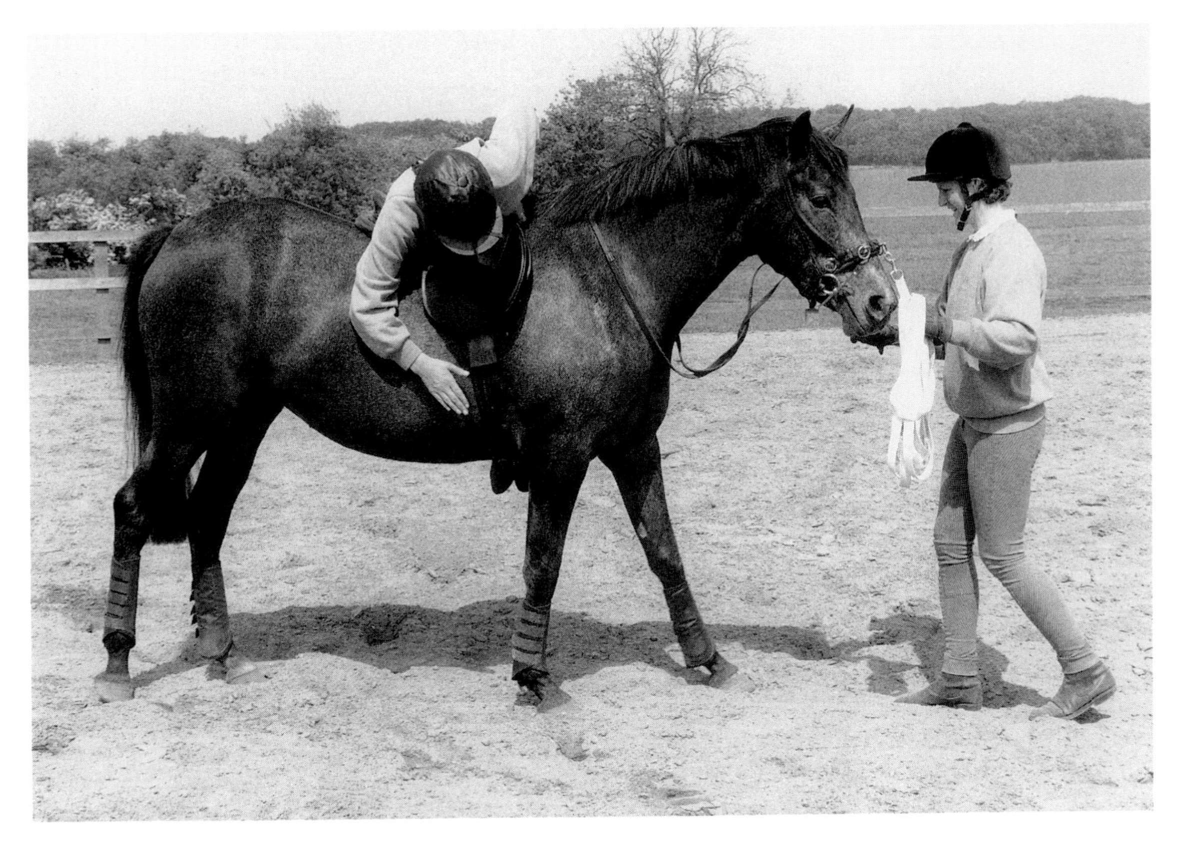

63 *(Above)* The rider slips her right leg over the saddle and gently sits in place

64 *(Left)* When mounted and being led for the first time, it is essential that the rider does not come off, so the stirrups are used to provide security and to help with balance in case the horse does play up

Fig. 28 *(Right)* The horse should be walked around on a short lunge line at first, until it is gradually played out and the horse is lungeing properly. The rider is still a passenger and the trainer controls the horse

surprises. The rider assumes a totally passive role, and is in fact simply a passenger at this stage. He or she follows the horse's movements, but does not give any aids. It is the person leading who controls the horse.

Once the horse has walked a little way, halt and make much of him. Then walk on again, halt and reward him again. Repeat this on both reins.

Within a few days, you will be able to begin lungeing the horse with the rider on top. Start by keeping the horse on a short lunge line, and simply walk and halt as before. The rider is still a passenger at this stage, and does not give legs aids or use the reins **(fig. 28)**.

Trotting

Once the horse is accustomed to walking on the lunge with a rider on his back, trotting can commence. The rider should take hold of the reins at this point. Although the control of the horse still rests with the person lungeing, the rider may need to use the reins to keep the horse's head up. If allowed to put their heads down towards their forelegs, some horses will try to buck.

The rider should always rise to the trot, so as not to put undue strain on the horse's back. The rider should keep his or her weight forward, and sit as lightly as possible in the saddle.

The worst thing that most horses try to do at this stage is to give a buck, so both trainer and rider must try to anticipate this. With a young horse this is not too difficult, as he will try to get his head down and arch his back – an action that is immediately apparent. Before the horse has accomplished this, you should have recognized the signs. The trainer immediately sends the horse on into a more active trot, with the lungeing whip if necessary, and the rider gives the voice command 'teerot'. This will divert the horse's attention and prevent the buck from being carried out.

THE IMPORTANCE OF PRACTICE

- At first, simply repeat and confirm what you have taught the horse. During his short ridden sessions, he should be mounted and dismounted regularly from both sides, and walked and trotted on both reins.
- The horse must not do any work in canter at this stage, as he is still too immature for this to serve any purpose and you will risk him tripping and falling.
- In order not to confuse the horse, you must allow him time to become used to the rider's weight and movement on his back, before he can be expected to learn the use of the rider's aids. You should therefore carry on in this way for two weeks or so.
- When first carrying the weight of a rider the horse will tire easily, so sessions need to be built up gradually.
- Stick to the principle of keeping the horse's work varied: on some days you should lunge and ride him for a short time; on other days you might long rein him and not ride him at all; and another day you might loose school and then ride him.

Standing to be mounted

One extremely important lesson which should be learned at this stage is standing still for mounting and dismounting. There is nothing more tiresome than a horse which continually tries to move off before the rider is in the saddle, and if the lesson is not learned at this stage, it becomes increasingly more difficult to teach as time goes by.

The horse must learn to stand while the rider takes up the reins, places the foot in the stirrup and mounts. Many riders do not now mount using the stirrups, preferring to use a mounting block or have a leg-up, because it is felt that continually mounting from the ground puts an unnatural strain on the back. The horse must be taught to accept this way of mounting, however, as there may come a time when the rider has to use this method – if he or she has had to dismount out on a hack, for instance.

The horse should remain stationary once the rider is in the saddle, and should remain so until an aid to move off has been given. This is to enable the stirrups and girth to be altered safely if necessary.

If the horse tries to move off each time he is to be mounted, the rider must insist on obedience by taking up the rein and using the familiar command 'stanD', with the emphasis on the 'D'. This should be repeated as many times as is necessary to ensure that the horse stands still. The rider should *not* mount and then try to make the horse halt.

If the horse persists in moving before the rider is mounted, an intermediate stage can be used, by standing someone directly in front of the horse to act as a barrier. Standing the horse in front of a wall is not such a good idea, as he will then have to be pulled round before he can move off.

This lesson might take a little time to accomplish, but is a valuable one which will benefit any rider of the horse, whenever he is ridden.

Acceptance of the legs

Once the horse is lungeing well with a passenger on top, it is time to teach him to respond to the rider's aids and control, in readiness for riding off the lunge. To this end, the rider firstly takes more control by making verbal requests himself rather than relying on the trainer. At the same time, the rider should gradually begin to take up a light contact on the reins, and to apply slight leg pressure when required. These aids are re-affirmed by the trainer using the body position and whip, but not verbally. Too much talk will only confuse the horse.

The horse which has been well long reined will soon connect the pressure through the reins and the feel of pressure on his sides by the rider with his earlier teachings, and so tends to learn what is required more quickly. The rider should carry a schooling whip at this stage to reinforce the leg aids when necessary. The horse must learn to move on when slight pressure is applied: nothing is worse than seeing a horse being continually kicked because he has never learned to move away from the leg properly.

Once the horse is being controlled by the rider, he can begin to work off the lunge line **(fig. 29)**. The work will be the same as before: that is, walking, trotting, standing, changing the rein, mounting and dismounting, but now the rider will be in charge **(65** and **66)**. Once the horse has accepted being backed, and being controlled by the rider on his back, he can be quietly hacked out to get him used to new sights and sounds and to keep him interested and happy.

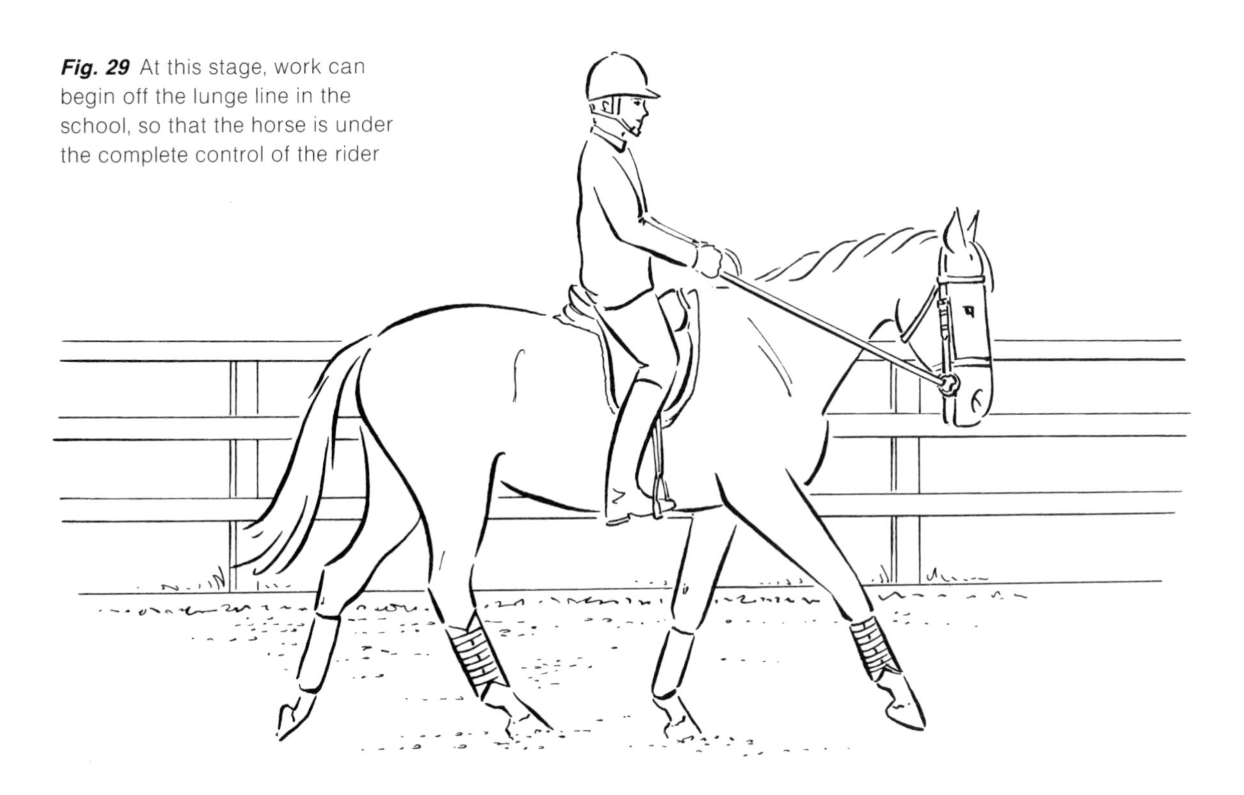

Fig. 29 At this stage, work can begin off the lunge line in the school, so that the horse is under the complete control of the rider

Familiarity and the benefits of a sensible lead horse

As stressed throughout this book, familiarity is a great aid to training horses. They are more settled in known surroundings, and, being creatures of habit, do not take well to too much change. Horses are also natural herd creatures, and you can make use of this in your training by enlisting the help of an older, more experienced lead horse.

This older 'nanny' horse – which must have a calm temperament – can be introduced into the school while the youngster is lungeing or long reining. Allow the youngster to make friends with the horse, and to follow him for certain exercises. You should also request the youngster to work with him in sight, and expect him to obey you and not become distracted by his 'nanny'. The youngster may follow his nanny when first mounted and from then on in various sessions, but should also be required to work alone.

The older horse will be of great benefit when first hacking out **(67)**, as he will be less likely to spook at silly things and will be well-behaved in traffic – an example that the youngster should soon learn to follow.

Turning away

Once he has been backed, there is little more that the young horse can learn at this stage. If you try to go straight into the second elementary stage of ridden work, you will risk mental and physical damage to the horse. For about six weeks after the horse is backed, you should therefore not teach anything new, and merely carry on reinforcing the ridden, lungeing, loose-schooling and long-reining lessons previously carried out.

65 *(Left)* When first riding the horse, you must continue using voice aids while introducing the leg and hand aids (*note:* how the horse's ears are listening to the rider, and he looks ready to comply with any request)

66 *(Above)* You should always be one step ahead, and ready to react if the horse 'naps', as here. In this situation, as the horse does not yet know what the rider's legs are for, the rider should use her voice and the trainer should assist if necessary to encourage the horse forward

67 *(Right)* An older 'nanny' horse will be of great benefit when first hacking out the youngster

At the end of this period it is hoped that you will have established a sound level of communication with your horse, based on trust. You should also have a confident and sensible youngster by this time, which is sufficiently balanced when both ridden and unridden.

The horse can now be turned away for a time, to allow him to mature both physically and mentally before the second stage of more serious schooling work commences. If you started your youngster in the spring of his third year, he would probably be sufficiently strong and developed to come back into work in the autumn. It is not unusual, however, to leave less well-developed youngsters until the spring of their fourth year.

Monty Roberts's advance-and-retreat technique

Monty Roberts, a Californian trainer, has given some fascinating demonstrations of his unique method of 'starting' horses. This has, in the 1990s, altered the way in which many people view the more traditional methods of 'breaking in' in the UK. It was Queen Elizabeth II who first invited Monty Roberts to England in 1989 and, after witnessing his revolutionary way of starting horses, has since directed her staff to use his methods on her problem horses.

His methods have been based on a lifetime's study of equine communication, and provide some valuable insights into horse psychology. Monty Roberts aims to replace the suspicion of humans that a halter-broken, but otherwise un-handled, youngster might have, by an overpowering curiosity and desire to approach humans, resulting in a willingness to be saddled and ridden away. The remarkable aspect of his method is that it takes – on average – less than half an hour to accomplish.

It is easily apparent that, within a very short space of time, a bond is formed between Monty Roberts and the horse he is starting. His control over a horse which he has never seen before appears almost hypnotic, but in fact he is communicating with the horse through an intense concentration of mind, eye contact and body language, which 'bonds' with the horse rather than dominating it.

He insists, however, that this is a transferable technique, and has in fact shown this to be the case. After he had given only a few hours' tuition to volunteers earlier in the day, they were able to go on and demonstrate his methods successfully themselves.

Although traditional methods also aim to establish trust and confidence in young horses, Monty Roberts believes that many traditionally broken horses form an adversarial relationship with their trainers, and only perform for them with a reluctant attitude. His theory is that the horse, as a quintessential flight animal, will always choose to flee rather than fight, and he has therefore developed what is known as the 'advance-and-retreat' technique.

The Monty Roberts procedure

When the 'raw' youngster is first led into the starting enclosure Monty Roberts gently rubs his forehead. He then moves away to the rear of the horse, but not close enough to be kicked, and sends the horse forward around the ring by the flick of a loose rein and body language; he never uses a whip. The body language used is one which he feels corresponds to the way in which horses square up to each other naturally. By standing with his shoulders square to the horse's head, he never loses eye contact for a second.

He never hits the horse, and simply

keeps him moving with a flick of the loose rein now and again. To change the rein, he simply swaps the loose rein from one hand to the other, which sends the horse off in the opposite direction.

He waits for the moment when he feels that the horse has had enough, which he recognizes by observing the horse's ears, and then assumes a 'submissive' mode, by casting his eyes down and therefore breaking the eye contact so vital earlier. He then turns his shoulders at a 45° angle to the horse, as an invitation for him to turn in and 'advance'. This moment is called 'join-up'. He then moves away from the horse and – sometimes immediately, or sometimes after repeating the process a few times – the horse follows him around like a dog.

Bridling, saddling and then backing and riding away in walk, trot and canter on each rein follows, and within thirty minutes or so from beginning to end the horse has been 'started'. It is clear from this that the other essential ingredient to Monty's success lies in doing everything very quickly, so as not to allow the horse time to react negatively.

There is no doubt that Monty Roberts's methods, which are carried out in a circular 15 m (50 ft) diameter enclosure with 2.5 m (8 ft) sides and a sandy flooring, work under controlled circumstances and under expert guidance. It is therefore well worth bearing his teachings in mind when training youngsters. Even if an individual is not experienced enough or does not have the facilities to make use of such methods, they do give a valuable insight into horse psychology.

This is not a technique without hazard, however, and is not a method recommended for anyone without a great deal of experience and understanding of youngsters. Above all, it should be recognized that Monty Roberts's intuitive approach is based on a lifetime study of equine communication and behaviour and, without such knowledge and understanding, it would be hard to emulate such a master.

KEY POINTS

- Backing can begin when the horse is obedient to the trainer on the lunge and in long reins, which will be, on average, about two months after the starting process has begun.
- It is dangerous to attempt to back a horse for the first time on your own, and so an assistant must be on hand at this stage.
- The horse should be backed in his normal working area, which he already associates with obedience to training requests.
- When mounted and being led for the first time, it is essential that the rider does not fall off.
- Standing still for mounting and dismounting is an extremely important lesson for the horse to learn.
- Once the horse is lungeing well with a passenger on top, it is time to teach him to respond to the rider's aids and control, in readiness for riding off the lunge.
- Familiarity is a great aid to training horses.
- Having been backed and ridden on for approximately six weeks, the horse should be turned away to mature mentally and physically.
- Monty Roberts's intuitive approach to 'starting' horses is based on a lifetime study of equine communication and behaviour.

Part 3

ADVANCED TRAINING

8

FOLLOWING UP

Re-backing

If your youngster has developed well and matured over the summer months, he may be brought back up in the autumn to benefit from a period of hacking out before schooling work commences in the spring. As has already been mentioned, the less-developed horse will benefit more from being turned away all through the winter to start work as a four-year-old. Although he is turned away, you should still bring the horse in to be fed and checked over every day. You should also lead and groom him, and pick out his feet, so that he retains his obedience and stable manners.

Once you decide to start riding your horse again, you should ensure that you have time to work him every day. Establishing a routine of work is very important at this stage, as it is in this year that you will be setting the foundations which will apply for the rest of the horse's life. Total commitment is needed for schooling a youngster.

Before you can progress to any kind of elementary training, you need to reinforce what the horse has already learned by repeating the lungeing and long-reining training and the backing procedure carried out the previous year. This will be accomplished far more quickly this time, as you are simply re-establishing what the horse already knows.

Once the horse is back at the stage at which you finished the previous year, you can move on. Some horses will benefit from a few weeks' hacking out before schooling commences, especially if they lack natural, free forward motion **(fig. 30)**. If you will be hacking out on the road, the horse should wear exercise and knee boots for protection **(fig. 31)**.

Your aims at this stage are to develop the horse's muscles and to work on him becoming more supple throughout his back and neck, which will benefit his overall health and fitness. You will achieve this by using structured exercises, which will enable the horse to work in the correct outline for this stage of training. In order to accomplish this, you will need to make him more responsive to your leg, hand and seat aids.

The aids

You will not accomplish a great deal if the horse does not know what you are asking. You therefore need to show him what you want him to do by the use of aids, and he will have to learn these before you can communicate fully. Rather than thinking in terms of aids to go forward or backward,

Fig. 30 A few weeks' hacking out before schooling starts may be beneficial

it is often easier to think in terms of *upward* and *downward* aids. If you give an upward aid, the horse must learn to move on; a downward aid and he needs to slow down.

The voice

You will already have used this concept in your verbal commands when training in-hand. To ask the horse to go on, you used a brisk, light tone in varying degrees to alter the pace, and to slow the pace, you used lower tones spoken in a more soothing manner. Carry on with these while introducing the leg and hand aids, so that the horse has some idea of what you mean.

The legs

The leg aids should be taught in stages. Firstly, you must establish the aid to go forward, which is the fundamental aid. You can then concentrate on the more delicate aids for creating the bend or downward transitions.

The aid to ask for forward movement is an inward push and a squeeze on the girth, accompanied at this initial stage by the

Fig. 31 Exercise boots and knee boots suitable for walking work on the road. Over-reach boots may also be a good idea, depending on your horse's action

verbal command to walk on. The rein must be free and unrestrained. If necessary, you should repeat the aid a few times, before strengthening it if the horse ignores it.

To strengthen the leg aid for forwardness, use the schooling whip just behind the girth at the exact moment of giving the aid. The aid that you give must be positive and momentary. Do not 'nag' with the leg, as the horse will simply switch off. If you need to repeat the aid, re-apply the leg, together with a smart tap of the whip, so that the horse realizes that he has not given the correct response the first time.

Repeat this throughout the lesson whenever you ask for forwardness. The horse must learn to react instantly and positively, although you should bear in mind that the young horse will take longer to interpret the aid and balance himself to carry it out than the more experienced horse. You are trying to reach a stage at which the leg aid is needed, without reinforcement from whip or voice.

The hands

Once the horse is moving forward from the leg, you will aim to control him between leg and hand. This is achieved by pushing the horse up into the hand, not by collecting him to the leg. The contact must be taken by the horse, not by you, or the horse will associate the pressure on the rein with not going forward.

The horse has to learn to recover his natural balance under the weight of a rider, and he usually accomplishes this first in trot. It is therefore at this pace that you will first find the horse seeking a contact with the bit by stretching down his head and neck. Until the horse starts to take this contact of his own accord, you must keep the reins long with only the slightest contact in all paces.

At this stage you will only use either a long rein or a slack rein. A long rein is where the horse can find a contact by striding long and low, reaching for the bit by stretching his neck. A slack rein is used when the horse is being given a rest period between exercises, where the rein is actually drooping without any contact on the mouth at all.

The seat

At first the seat plays a very minor role, gently following the horse's movement in rhythm with his paces. The first time the seat is used with any real purpose is when you ask the horse to halt. As you do not want to use undue pressure on the reins, simply stop following the horse's movement and sit still, in order to transmit the lack of forward motion.

Free forward movement

In order to be able to move forward freely, the horse needs to be calm. His mental attitude will reflect in everything physical that he does, as tension in the mind instantly reflects in the muscles. If you have re-backed him well, you should have a horse which is full of trust in you and ready to learn. You can now go on to stimulate him mentally by offering new and exciting challenges.

One of the dangers of an inexperienced rider setting out to train a novice horse is that work tends to be carried out aimlessly and – although the horse may be ridden sensibly – he does not progress. If a keen but inexperienced rider acquires the knowledge of what needs to be accomplished, however, he or she can set out with a purpose in mind when schooling.

If the rider then accomplishes one stage before moving on, he or she will progress with the horse, and benefit him or herself as well. The danger lies in things going wrong and the inexperienced rider working alone, not knowing how to correct the problem, so the aim is to minimize mistakes by acquiring knowledge before proceeding.

The best way to obtain calmness is to occupy the horse's mind. You can do this by giving him simple exercises on which to concentrate, such as large circles, transitions and changes of direction. Once the horse starts to think about what he is doing, he will soon settle. You can then go on to ask him to move forward.

Free forward movement does not simply mean the horse moving in a forward direction. Most youngsters are quite idle and actually need to be urged on, so they are moving freely as opposed to lazily. Initially, the horse finds it difficult to move straight, and tends to wander and weave, so you need to ride positively forward, transmitting forward thinking at all times. Keep driving the horse up into the hand from behind to create energy, which will give you the forward impulsion required to move on to more demanding work.

Transitions

All transitions should be progressive: for example, not straight from canter to walk, but through trot. Transitions should not be abrupt, but should be carried out smoothly. If the horse does not respond at first, you should repeat the aid, not continue it.

Transitions can be made upward or downward. The important aspect is that the horse maintains rhythm of pace up until the gait is changed, and then establishes rhythm of pace in the new gait as soon as possible. All young horses need to be prepared – even set up – for transitions. To do this for an upward transition, you must ensure that enough impulsion has been created, so that the horse can obey without hollowing his back and throwing his head in the air.

You must ride into all downward transitions. Do not restrict the movement by pulling on the reins to slow the pace, as this will simply encourage the horse to stiffen his back. Instead, maintain your seat and use a slightly restraining hand, which, at the same time, allows the horse to move 'forward' into the slower pace.

Developing muscle

The horse needs to develop muscle in order to balance himself with the added weight of the rider on his back. This is best

THE OBJECTIVES OF ELEMENTARY TRAINING

At all times, you must bear in mind that you can only develop the natural abilities that the horse possesses, not create the abilities that you desire. Producing a well-schooled youngster is rather like building a good house. Set a firm foundation and build up each brick correctly, forming strong layers as you go, and the house will be a solid one. Lay a shallow base and follow with haphazard layers, and the house will fall down. In other words, if you carry out the elementary training of your young horse correctly, further levels will follow on smoothly. The aims of elementary training are:

- that the horse moves freely forward
- that he moves in a constant and regular rhythm
- that he learns to accept rider contact
- that he learns to relax his shoulders and engage his hindquarters
- that he learns to move straight
- that he starts to develop a degree of collection
- that all objectives are achieved through obedience and understanding, not force

achieved at this stage by the use of frequent transitions from one pace to another, ensuring that the horse is taking long, level strides in between.

The horse's back muscles will tire easily at first, so sessions still need to be kept short, with rest periods between exercises. If the horse is allowed a rest every time he performs an exercise correctly, he soon learns that a rest is a reward. This is an excellent way of helping the horse to relax his muscles between exercises, which lowers the risk of strains.

It is important not to over-do any exercise. Try a new exercise two or three times, then rest and go on to something that the horse already understands, before trying again later on. If you insist on getting everything right, before you end the lesson, you will make the horse sick of his training sessions, and unco-operative as a result.

As long as the horse continues to be correctly fed and well-groomed, you will soon start to see a change in his overall shape, as his muscles develop.

Establishing rhythm and correct paces

Rhythm is something that is personal to the horse, as every horse has a slightly different natural length of stride at each pace. In the horse's elementary schooling, you can work on establishing his natural rhythm by teaching him to move actively and freely.

You are an important ingredient in allowing your horse to develop his rhythm at each pace. Before you can alter the rhythm of any pace, however, you need to 'feel' how the horse is moving, and work within those limits, rather than pushing the horse out of his rhythm in your haste to create impulsion. You must therefore start by working slowly, establishing a nice easy rhythm at first and then building on it once you are in harmony with the horse.

The important factor is that the horse learns to be consistent with rhythm, and does not rush round corners or idle along

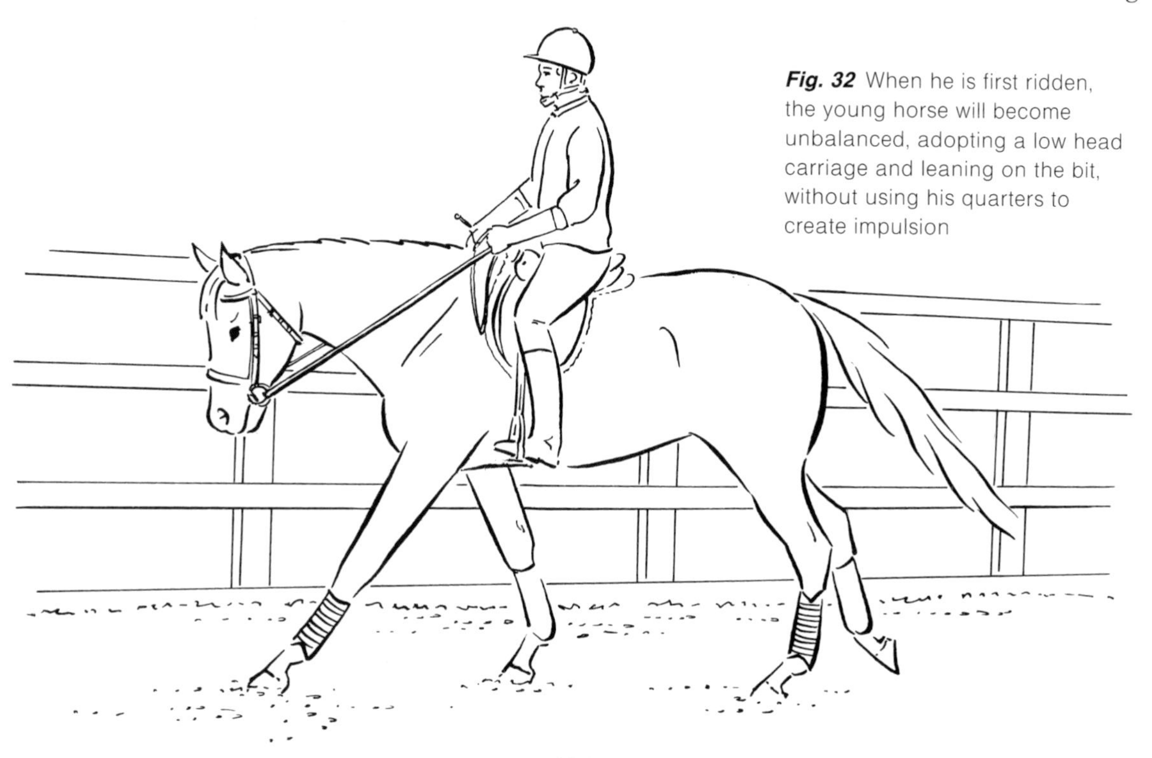

Fig. 32 When he is first ridden, the young horse will become unbalanced, adopting a low head carriage and leaning on the bit, without using his quarters to create impulsion

the side of the school. To be able to maintain rhythm of pace, the horse must be balanced, and here you must consider our own ability. You should be aware of the timing of each pace, knowing that the walk is a four-time movement, the trot a two-time movement and the canter a six-eight movement. As you ride your horse you can actually count the beats, and this is beneficial when establishing rhythm with a young horse. You need to adapt to the movement of each pace in order to help the horse work in balance.

The young horse will become unbalanced when first ridden, taking most of your weight on his forehand **(fig. 32)**. As training progresses, you need to help the horse change the balance so that more weight is carried by the hindquarters, giving him more freedom to extend.

In order to do this, you need to make the horse more supple through the back by working long and low, and concentrating on creating an easy rhythm. Once this is established, you can then work on asking the horse to bring his quarters under him, and therefore re-distributing your weight, which will enable him to achieve better balance.

Throughout, you need to feel the movement of the horse and to keep in harmony with him as he progresses. Once you can feel that the horse has achieved better balance and a regular rhythm, you can go on to ask for more expression in the paces and to add cadence.

Exercises

In the early stages of training the horse is only required to carry out simple exercises, such as figures, changes of pace and direction, and also moving in straight lines, which is not as easy for the horse as you might imagine. The figures that you ride should be executed accurately: for example, circles should be round (not oval), serpentines should be regular, and, of course, lines should be straight **(fig. 33)**. It is important not to work on too small a diameter when riding figures. Circles should be no smaller than 20 m (65 ft) at this stage: half-circles no smaller than approximately 15 m (49 ft) and loops in a serpentine no smaller than about 12 m (39 ft) in diameter.

The horse is naturally crooked, and so you will have to straighten him. By doing so, you will actually have to alter his natural way of going, which is done by working equally on both reins, to develop both sides of the horse evenly. Most people appreciate that a horse goes better on one rein than another (usually the left), but do not realize that there is a physical reason for this. Just as the majority of humans are right-handed, so the majority of horses are left-sided.

Work at straightening the natural movement of the horse one step at a time, by using these simple exercises, and gauge your results by whether the horse tracks up (whether his hind footprints fall directly over his fore footprints), or not.

Straightness is fundamental to any horse's training, whether his ability eventually proves him to be a dressage star or a show jumper. The purpose of all the basic exercises that you use at this stage is therefore to improve suppleness throughout the neck and back, resulting in straightness, which will in turn help rhythm and balance.

The worst mistake in riding exercises of this nature is to ask for and to control the bend with the inside hand. If you do this, the horse will use your inside hand as a balancing aid, and will not support himself by using his inside hind leg. The *outside* hand is the balancing rein, which will control the impulsion created by your inside leg. You must therefore always work the horse from your inside leg into

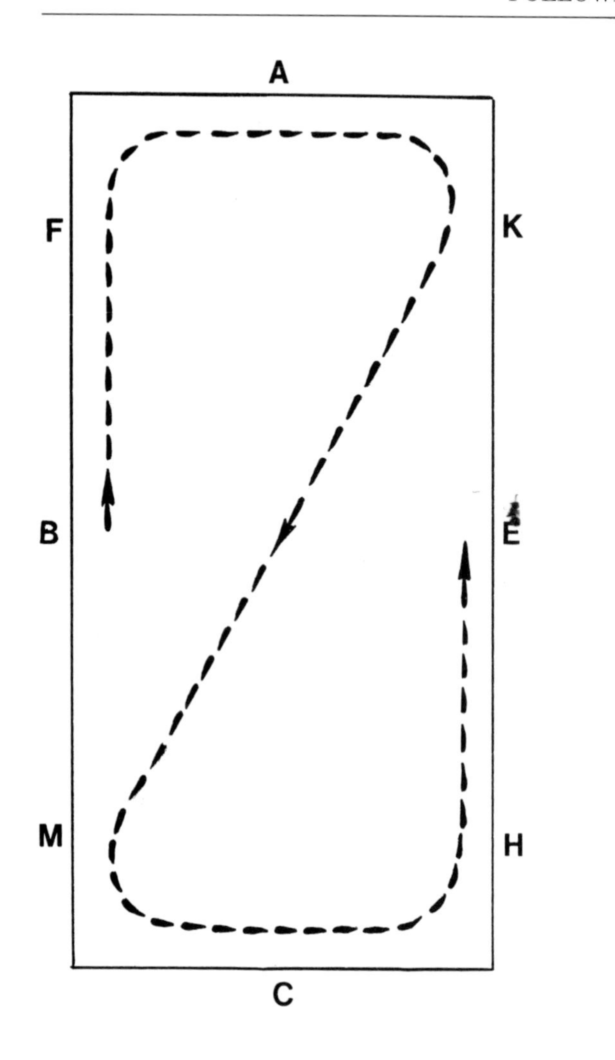

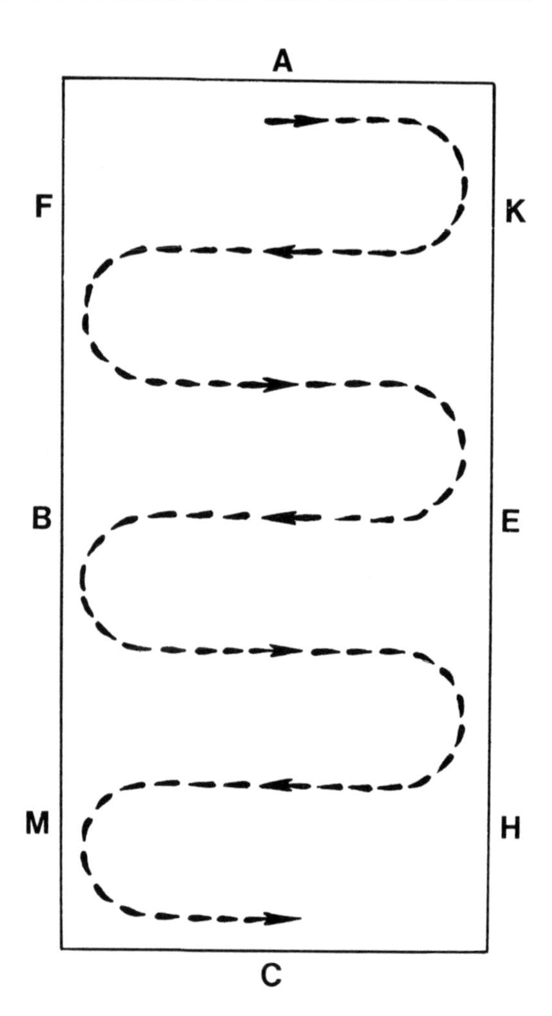

Fig. 33 Some of the simple figures used in basic training

your outside hand, in order to prevent the horse from swinging out his quarters and losing 'straightness'.

Working through

Many trainers talk about 'putting the horse on the bit', which is another term often misunderstood. It seems to conjure up all sort of ideas of positioning the horse's head in a certain way, by some magical use of the reins. Putting the horse on the bit is in fact something which develops naturally through correct training, and is not some sort of head carriage achieved by pulling on the reins at all.

I therefore prefer to talk about contact with the bit and working in the correct outline, collectively known as 'working through'. Once the horse has sought contact with the bit as previously described (see page 88), you can then go on to influence the horse to move to the best of his ability.

To do this you will use leg, seat and hand aids, which all work in co-ordination. Work the horse in trot on a large circle, maintaining a light, steady but firm contact, and then ask for relaxation in the

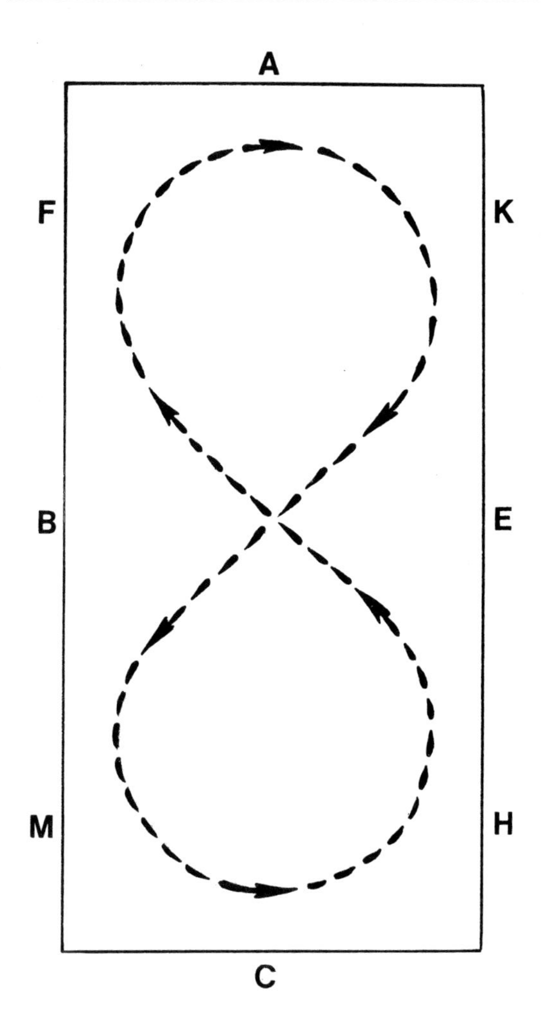

back and neck by thinking forward and low. Lastly, ask the horse to 'step forward' into the outline by using your legs to bring his quarters underneath him, while maintaining the firm, steady contact. All this is accomplished without losing forward impulsion, and by maintaining rhythm. You must think of working from the quarters, over the horse's back into your hands, in order to put the horse into the correct outline – not in terms of working from the bit backward.

The physical appearance of the horse's outline is a less-accurate measure than the feel that you are experiencing. As you cannot experience 'working through' unless you are on a horse, however, the physical appearance is probably the best guide to those who have never experienced it.

The horse is said to be 'working through' when his hocks are well under him, with the power generated from his quarters being conducted forward into a light and steady contact from bit to hand. This is most apparent by the head and neck position, which is raised from the withers and flexed at the poll, with the head in a steady position, slightly in front of the vertical, with a relaxed jaw.

Once the horse is working through in this way, you have really achieved something. The horse is showing that he is perfectly ready to comply with your requests, and is absolutely willing and happy to do so.

When you have achieved this state of harmony with your horse, you must be careful not to abuse it by asking too much. The horse will find this work physically and mentally demanding, as he will be holding himself together in readiness for the slightest aid, while at the same time maintaining active, rhythmic strides and concentrating on the exercises that he has been requested to perform.

You must therefore allow the horse to rest frequently by offering him a loose rein, and should only build up gradually to the ultimate aim of having the horse 'working through' at all times (unless on a loose rein).

Further exercises

Once the horse has learned the aids for upward and downward transitions, you can introduce him to more subtle aids. Until this point, you have concentrated on establishing balanced paces, but, by the use of various exercises, you can now begin to introduce a few schooling 'movements'.

At this stage, you should restrict these movements to the halt, half-halt and turn on the forehand. More advanced movements do not really apply to the basic training of the young horse, and so are not covered in this book.

The halt

At first, more emphasis should be put on the horse actually standing still, once halted, than on him standing squarely. You should build up the length of time he is still gradually, until he is able to stand attentively for about five seconds. Once this is achieved, you can begin asking him to halt squarely, so that his weight is evenly distributed on all four legs, with both forelegs and hind legs parallel with each other. This is achieved by having plenty of impulsion as you come into the halt, so that the weight is taken on to the hindquarters.

The half-halt

This is used to increase activity, by stopping the horse from simply increasing speed when driving aids are applied. By giving tactful but firm driving aids, together with a momentary restraint on the rein, you will increase the horse's balance and attention, and therefore help to engage the quarters by generating impulsion which lightens the forehand.

You need to aim for the stage at which you can hold the horse together with seat and leg aids, without reliance on the rein. As training progresses, the half-halt becomes more useful.

The turn on the forehand

This is where the horse's quarters rotate around his forehand **(fig. 34)**. It is used in basic training to increase suppleness in the back, and is a good introduction to lateral aids. The bend normally created is away from the direction of the movement, but it can be towards the direction of the movement.

To perform from a halt to move left, apply the right leg behind the girth and take a firm contact on the right rein, to encourage a slight bend in that direction at the poll.

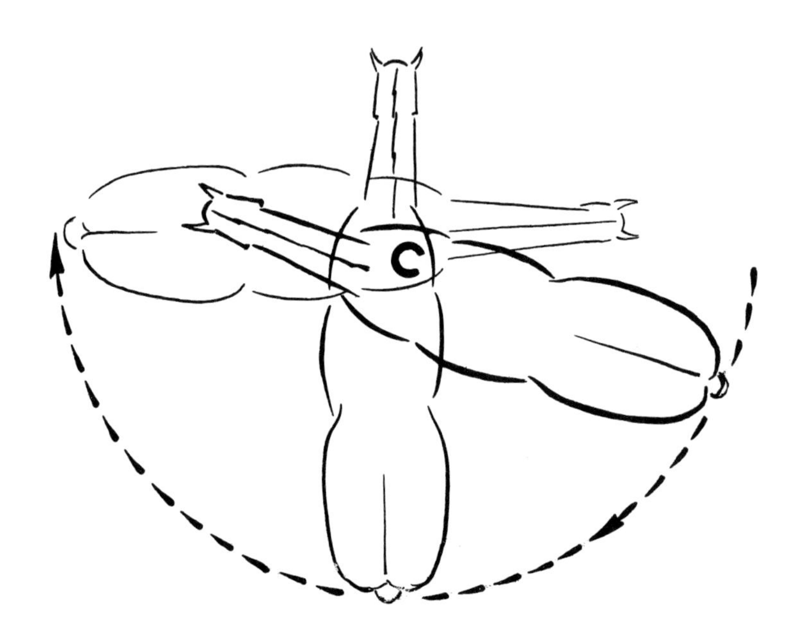

Fig. 34 The turn on the forehand

AVOIDING BOREDOM

- Although you need to repeat exercises and lessons to establish them fully in the horse's mind, you must be careful to vary his work as much as possible within lessons and with work periods themselves.
- The horse does not need to be schooled in the working area every day, and so you can take him out on hacks, as well as continuing with work in-hand, to avoid boredom **(68)**.
- Much of your schooling work can be reinforced on hacks. You will be performing upward and downward transitions, making changes in direction and giving aids without the horse even thinking of it as 'work'.
- The more you can do to vary the horse's workload, the more content you will make him in his work, and the more experience he will gain without becoming sour.

Work in canter

Once you have the horse moving freely forward in balance, and he can maintain that balance around the bend by supporting himself and not leaning on the inside rein (as discussed on page 125), you can commence cantering work.

When you first ask for canter, you want the horse to strike off on the correct leading leg. You must therefore only ask for canter at an appropriate time, by using one end of the working area and asking for canter when you are coming into the corner. To ask for canter, first establish an active trot on the circle, with the horse working through. When this is being

68 Continuing with work in-hand, both in the school and outside it, will add variety and help to prevent boredom

performed well, with the horse balanced and attentive, sit for a few beats when approaching the corner, and give the leg aid for forwardness on the inside girth. At the same time, apply the outside leg behind the girth and relax the inside rein, while holding firm and steady the contact on the outside rein.

If you have timed this well, the horse will lead off into canter on the correct leg, and you should then ride him for one or two circuits in canter on a light rein before slowing him gently into trot. If he does not strike off on the correct leg, slowly bring him back into trot and try again. Do not rush the horse, and be sure to re-establish a nice, balanced trot before trying again. After one or two attempts, the horse will usually get the idea. If he still has trouble, however, you should go on to something else before trying again. On no account should you ask the horse to perform the trot–canter transition unless he is completely relaxed.

Try another trot–canter transition on the opposite rein. If the horse is happy to strike off into canter, again complete a few circuits and then slowly ask for trot. If the horse has some difficulty, then he is probably still more stiff on one side than another, and you should carry out more suppling and straightening work before repeating the exercise.

After the first few canters, where you are merely letting the horse experience the pace with a rider on his back, you can start to work the pace. To do this, work equally on both reins, performing upward and downward transitions on large circles. This will help the horse to relax, enabling him to 'work through' by engaging his hind legs and establishing a light contact with the rein. He should then have no trouble in consistently striking off on the correct lead.

It is a mistake to try to throw the horse on to the correct leg by rushing him into the corner and turning his head inward – something one often sees novice riders doing. The horse will simply become unbalanced, and – although the correct lead may be achieved – he will not be able to maintain the pace for very long and may become disunited.

Developing fitness

The young horse does not need to be extremely fit. Indeed, if he is too fit this will hamper progress, as he will become very full of himself. As work progresses, however, he is bound to become fitter. By the end of his first six months after re-backing, he should be sufficiently schooled to cope with being fitter, and be feeling the joys of life. His mental attitude will also have developed to such an extent that he knows when it is permissible to have a little fun, and when it is necessary for him to settle into his work.

His elementary training is now drawing to its conclusion, and most riders will want to start training for a specific purpose: show jumping, dressage or eventing, perhaps. The horse's condition and fitness will gradually need to build up in order to cope with the more advanced training that will be required.

Most of this fitness work will be done out hacking, where you can use the natural terrain – especially hills – to your benefit. Firstly, you should increase the amount of trotting that you do in each session aiming for two ten-minute sessions with a good break in between, within a one-hour period. You should then build up canter work, using slow canter work to build up stamina and faster sprints to enhance breathing **(fig. 35)**. Each individual horse will take different lengths of time to reach the same level of fitness, so the rule here should be to stop when the horse has had enough, but to know your

Fig. 35 Canter work should be built up gradually to increase fitness

horse well enough to understand when to ask for that extra bit more. Allow the horse to steadily lengthen into a gallop at times, when the weather and terrain permit.

Preventing bad habits

Working correctly requires a great deal of effort on the horse's part, and so any horse will evade going correctly if he can, and any youngster will soon pick up bad habits if he is permitted to do so.

Never under-estimate the intelligence of the horse. Although you may have laid the correct foundations in your earlier training, the horse will use his intelligence to try to avoid situations that he finds difficult. Hopefully, you will have such a rapport with your horse by this stage that you will know if he is avoiding something because he finds it too difficult – in which case you have probably asked too much too soon – or because he is misbehaving.

As it is so much more difficult to correct problems than not to allow them to develop in the first place, you should always be on the look out for evasions of any kind. Any shortcuts in the horse's training will usually manifest themselves in one problem or another later on in his schooling, so the more correct and unhurried his early training, the less likelihood there will be of things going wrong.

Re-education

Although many people rise to the challenge of re-educating an older or spoilt horse, it is a demanding task. It can be fascinating – trying to work out exactly what the problem is, why it has been allowed to develop and how best to confront it in the hope of correcting or curing it – but it can be extremely difficult.

The horse will usually have to be taken right back to basics, and perhaps started all over again in the same way as a youngster. Once you are able to establish a level of communication with such a horse through the most effective method of punishment and reward, however, you may achieve a degree of success, if not total re-education and obedience.

KEY POINTS

- Even when turned away, the horse should still be brought in to be fed and checked over every day.
- Establishing a routine of work is very important at this stage, as it is in this year that you will be setting the foundations which will apply for the rest of the horse's life.
- The horse will need to learn the aids before you can communicate fully with him.
- The aid to go forward is the fundamental aid.
- Once the horse is moving forward from the leg, you should then aim to control him between your leg and hand. This is achieved by pushing the horse up into the hand, not by collecting the horse down to the leg.
- The best way to obtain calmness is to occupy the horse's mind.
- The horse's way of going is naturally crooked. You therefore have to straighten him, and by so doing, actually have to alter his natural way of going.
- When you first ask for canter, you want the horse to strike off on the correct leading leg. This is achieved by only asking for canter at an appropriate time.
- Any shortcuts in the horse's training will usually manifest themselves in to one problem or another later on in his schooling.

9

ADVANCED TRAINING FROM THE GROUND

Schooling on the lunge

Until this point, lungeing has been used with the aim of eventually riding the horse, but it can play a large part in the further training of the horse after he has been backed and ridden.

The objects of schooling on the lunge are the same as those when schooling mounted. You have already established obedience on the lunge, so you can now go on to develop the horse's outline and paces (as described on page 122–9), when he is being ridden. Once the paces are active on the lunge and the horse is working through from the hindquarters with a relaxed shoulder, you can start to vary the size of the circle and ask him to carry himself in a more advanced outline **(fig. 36)**.

To develop the 'rising' and 'lightening' required for a more rounded outline, you have to maintain the impulsion by keeping a constantly strong driving action. At the same time, you must keep a firm contact between cavesson and hand, which will play the rein by momentarily resisting and relaxing.

Fig. 36 At this stage of training, the horse is asked to develop a more 'rounded' as opposed to a 'long' outline

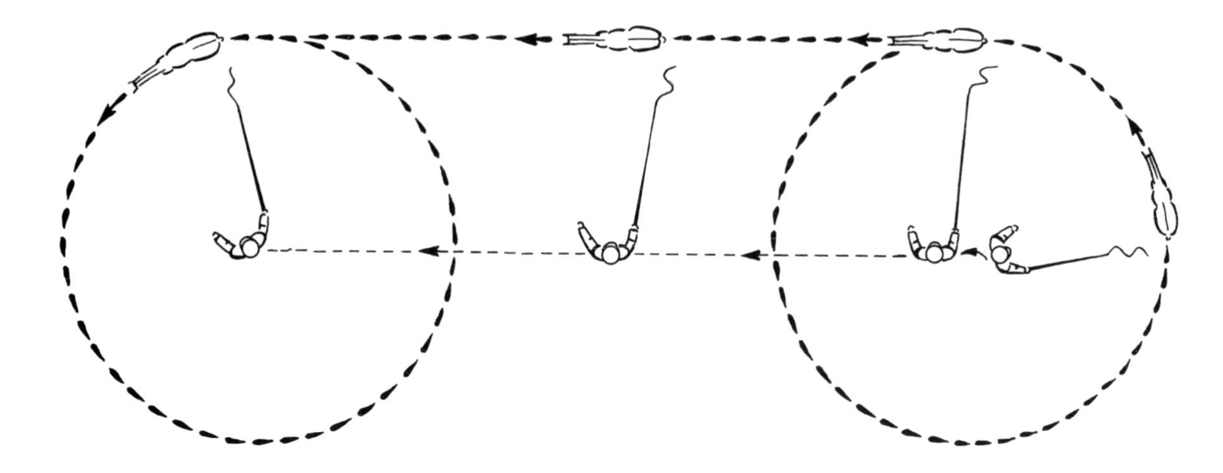

Fig. 37 Asking for extension on the lunge

All the gaits, as well as upward and downward transitions, can be performed on the lunge. Once they have been well established, you can consider variation in the form of increasing and decreasing the length of stride within each gait – referred to as *working*, *medium*, *collected* and *extended* paces.

Extension should not be attempted until a fair degree of collection has been obtained. To achieve such collection, you should work on gradually reducing the circle and then increasing it again in one exercise, being careful to go only as far as the horse's ability dictates at any one time. Some horses will be able to maintain rhythm and collection from 20 m (65 ft) to 10 m (33 ft) and back again. Others may only be able to maintain this down to 15 m (49 ft) and out again. Going too far will result in loss of rhythm and stiffness throughout the back, so you must be cautious and alert to the responses of each individual horse.

To ask for extension on the lunge, first establish an active, supple, collected pace on the circle. Push the horse out of the circle on to a straight line and drive for a few paces of extensions, following parallel with the horse as he goes. You should then resume a circle further up the working area **(fig. 37)**.

Reaching this stage of advanced training on the lunge will take time, and there are various books devoted to the whole subject. It may be that your horse is ready for more advanced work late in his fourth year, or not until his sixth year. It will all depend on his mental and physical attitude, on his training to date and on your abilities as a trainer. It does, however, give some idea of what can be achieved.

Lungeing and long-reining problems and evasions

It is a sad fact that most evasions occur through bad training and not through the fault of the horse alone. Although there are rogue horses, these are few and far between, and there are more bad trainers than bad horses.

One of the most common problems is over-work at too young an age, which strains muscles. The young horse consequently becomes stiff and sore, and the only way in which he can show his discomfort is by resisting. When you see such resistance in a horse, you have to decide whether he is in fact in some sort of pain, and so cannot settle, or whether he is being stubborn or lazy and refuses to settle because he simply does not want to work.

Other evasions include coming behind the bit or over the bit (see page 88). Again, these faults are often due to trainer error, such as fitting side reins too tightly too soon. To try to eliminate the possibility of such problems occurring, you should not take any shortcuts in the horse's training, however attractive quick results may seem. You should also eliminate resistance by making your requests easy for the horse to carry through.

You are likely to come across one form of resistance or another at some point, as you would be very lucky indeed if the horse complied exactly as you wished at the first time of asking **(69** and **70)**. He may object to something that you ask him to do or, at another time, he may try to challenge your authority. Whichever of these situations you come across, the important thing is to establish authority and insist that the horse complies – unless of course he is in pain or unwell.

The two most common problems on the lunge are as follows.

- The horse may object to changing the rein, and attempt to turn back round to the rein on which he was previously working. Alternatively, he may simply turn in and face the trainer. For the horse to be able to take advantage in this way, the trainer must have been away from his hip, and therefore not able to drive the horse on.

69 High jinks!

70 Here, the horse being asked to canter for the first time is trying to evade the trainer by bucking and fighting to get away

71 It may sometimes be necessary for an assistant to encourage the horse forward

To deal with this situation, the trainer should quietly walk up to the horse and fuss him so that he stands relaxed. The trainer then slowly moves towards the horse's hip, stroking him as he goes. Once in position, the trainer vigorously drives the horse forward by swishing the lunge whip along the ground while at the same time giving the rein, so that the horse can comply by moving forward, or – as he is likely to do in this situation – bound forward. The trainer must then be sure to maintain the driving position at the hip, or the horse will try to do it again. Alternatively, an assistant can be used to help in this situation **(71 and 72)**.

- The horse may switch off and carry on round the circle monotonously, ignoring his trainer's commands to stop. This

72 The whip is not used, but the horse complies

is due to a breakdown in communication somewhere along the line – usually because the trainer has bored the horse. The easiest way to deal with this is to put something in the horse's way – preferably a wall!

Instead of allowing the horse to continue on the circle, walk him straight until he walks straight up to the school wall or fence. This has the effect of making him 'snap out of it', and the session can be resumed or ended depending on how much work the horse has done. The trainer must then ensure that the horse is kept attentive at all times.

Trotting poles

Trotting poles are very useful in basic training. They can be used to:

- encourage the horse to lower his head and neck
- to help lengthen the stride
- to loosen and strengthen muscles
- to prepare the horse for jumping

You should only start work with poles once the horse has come through all the other stages, as previously described. Start by laying a single pole on one side of the lungeing track, and ask the horse to walk over it each time he comes to it. Then introduce another pole at the other side of the circle. Work over these in walk and trot until the horse steps over them quite calmly in his natural rhythm. In subsequent lessons, you can build up the poles on one side of the school into a grid of five or six poles, spaced approximately 1.5–2 m (5–6 ft) apart **(fig. 38)**.

The spacing of the poles is important, and you will need to adjust this to your horse's length of stride once he has been over them a few times. The horse must be able to work over the poles without having to alter his natural rhythm. He should

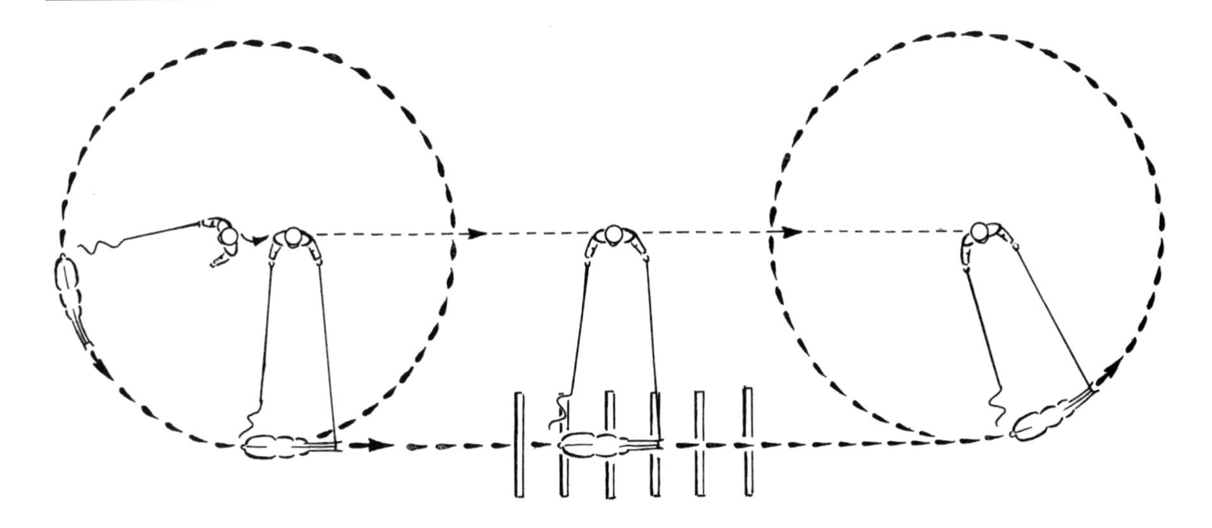

Fig. 38 Lungeing over a grid of poles

approach in a straight line and be allowed to go straight for a few strides after the poles, before being brought back on to the lungeing circle.

Once a smooth rhythm has been established over the grid, you can raise the poles off the floor by use of cavalletti or blocks at their lowest positions, to encourage greater activity.

Loose schooling over fences

Once the horse has learned to negotiate raised poles, work can begin over small fences. The best way to achieve this at first is to allow the horse to jump loose, so that he learns to negotiate the obstacles without hindrance, lengthening or shortening his stride as necessary on the approach **(fig. 39)**. In this way, loose jumping improves balance, co-ordination and athleticism. Most horses take to loose jumping readily, and really enjoy the sessions.

To loose jump safely, you need to use a securely fenced enclosure. This will ideally be partitioned into an oval jumping lane, with a track about 3.5 m (12 ft) wide. The outside of the track needs to be fairly high, so that the horse has no thought of jumping out. The inside of the track can be partitioned off with straw bales or hurdles, as with the field school.

The fences in the jumping lanes should be varied, including, for example, a brush fence, a ditch, a log, and other solid obstacles. It should also be easy to raise or

THE USE OF CAVALLETTI OR BLOCKS

- Some people prefer to use cavalletti rather than trotting poles, as they feel that horses soon learn to disregard poles on the ground and trip on them, risking strain to the legs. I feel that trotting poles are best at first, however, and that, once the initial aims have been reached, cavalletti work can commence.
- Many people are also now totally against the use of traditional cavalletti, as they feel that the crossed ends can be dangerous. As an alternative, the 'block' has been designed. This works on the same principle of allowing poles to be suspended at various heights, but they are constructed of solid plastic and are extremely safe.

lower them as necessary, and to remove altogether from the lane.

To start the horse loose jumping, first send him around the lane without any fences in it to allow him to loosen up and settle down. You should then introduce a jump of about 30 cm (1 ft) in height, and send the horse around the lane a few times in trot, exactly as you did in previous loose schooling sessions. The horse may rush the jump at first, but will soon settle into his rhythm and take it in his stride. Always start the horse in trot, and aim at regulating the pace throughout.

Once the horse has achieved a regular rhythm over the first jump, you can introduce another and then another over subsequent sessions until you have about four or five jumps. You can then start to raise one or two of the obstacles, to a maximum of 90 cm (3 ft). Parallels can also be widened until they are approximately 1.2 m (4 ft) wide.

You will often find that your horse becomes very enthusiastic, and it is up to you to reinforce the obedience that was required in the previous loose-schooling sessions, so that you can maintain a nice balanced rhythm throughout.

It is extremely important to use protective boots when loose jumping. Not only will the horse be more likely to knock and bang himself, but, without support, he will run the risk of striking up a splint.

Lungeing over fences

If you cannot construct a jumping lane, you can lunge the horse over fences in the same way. The horse should not jump on a circle, however, and you will need to be fit

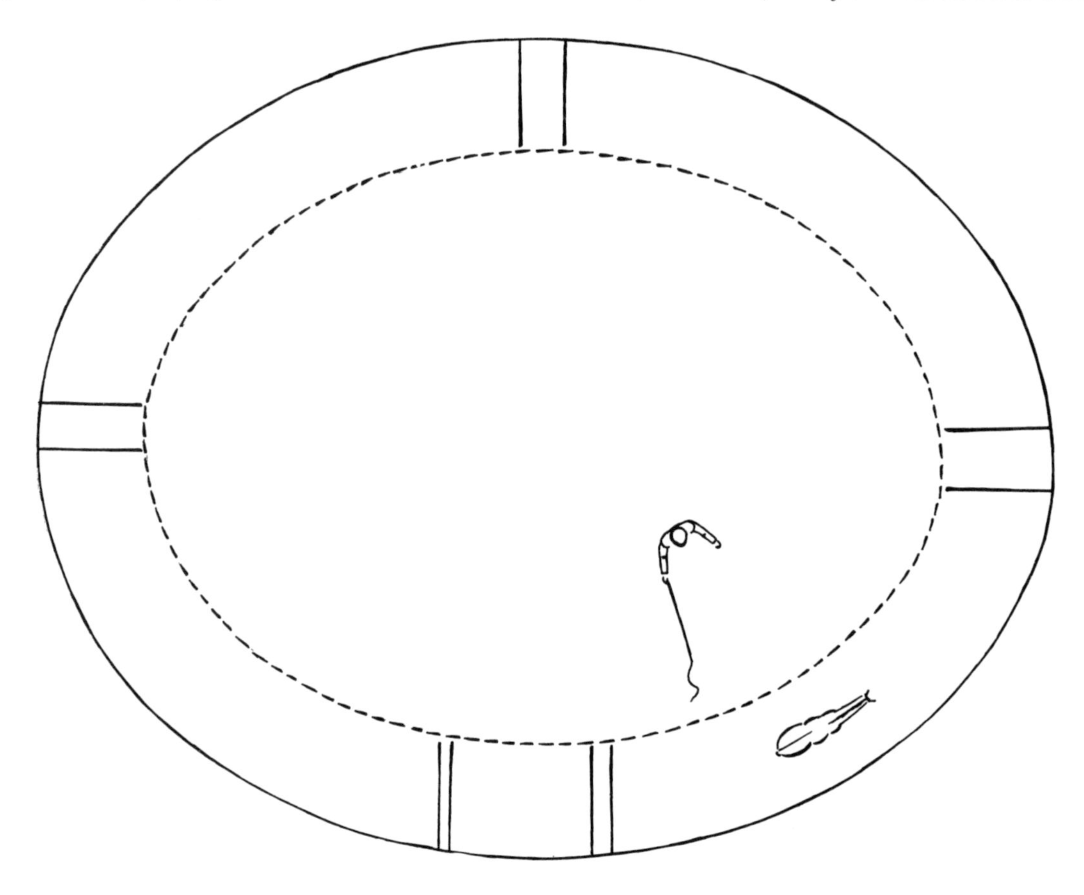

Fig. 39 A loose-jumping lane

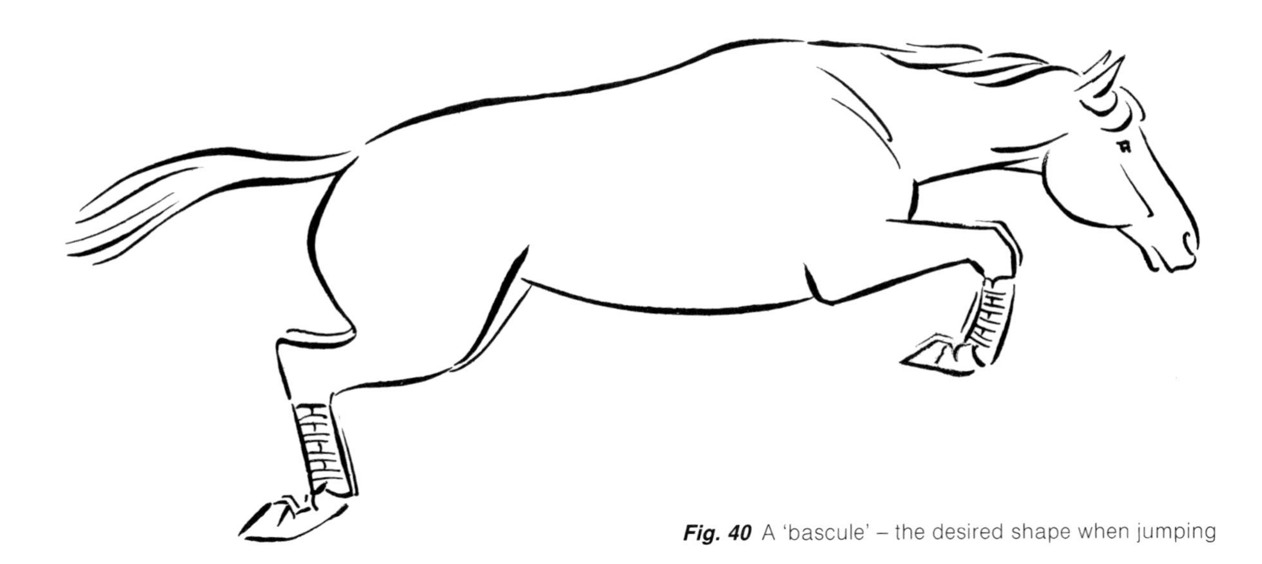

Fig. 40 A 'bascule' – the desired shape when jumping

yourself to keep up with him. Proceed in exactly the same way as with loose jumping, by building up the number, height and width of fences around the outside of the working area. It is not a good idea to attempt to lunge over fences in the open, and so, if a schooling area is not available, you should construct a makeshift area as described on pages 61–3.

Lungeing or loose schooling over fences should not be carried out every day, nor should the horse do more than a few circuits on each rein in any one session, or he will learn to rush in order to get to the end.

The idea of these jumping exercises is to get the horse to use himself to his best physical advantage. He should approach each fence calmly, learn to use his back, tuck up his legs and stretch his neck over the fence, and then make a soft landing and proceed calmly afterwards.

The term for making the correct shape over a fence is a *bascule*, and you should work to encourage this over any fence **(fig. 40)**. The correct style of jumping is best explained by saying that the horse makes a half-circle over the fence from the take-off to landing **(fig. 41)**. By observing from the ground how the horse jumps, you can therefore evaluate the 'shape' and the 'style', which gives a true advantage over the rider.

The construction of lungeing fences

When lungeing over fences, you need to be careful of their construction so that the lunge rein does not become caught. The safest method is to place the fence up against the outer fencing of the working area, with a pole resting from the uppermost part of the fence to the floor, on either side of the inner edge of the jump **(fig. 42)**.

Long reining over fences

It is also possible to long rein over fences, although this requires a skilful hand and a quick mind, and is not the easiest task to accomplish. It is therefore best to become accustomed to it by first using an older horse, which is used to the activity, before

Fig. 41 A half-circle – the desired 'style' when jumping

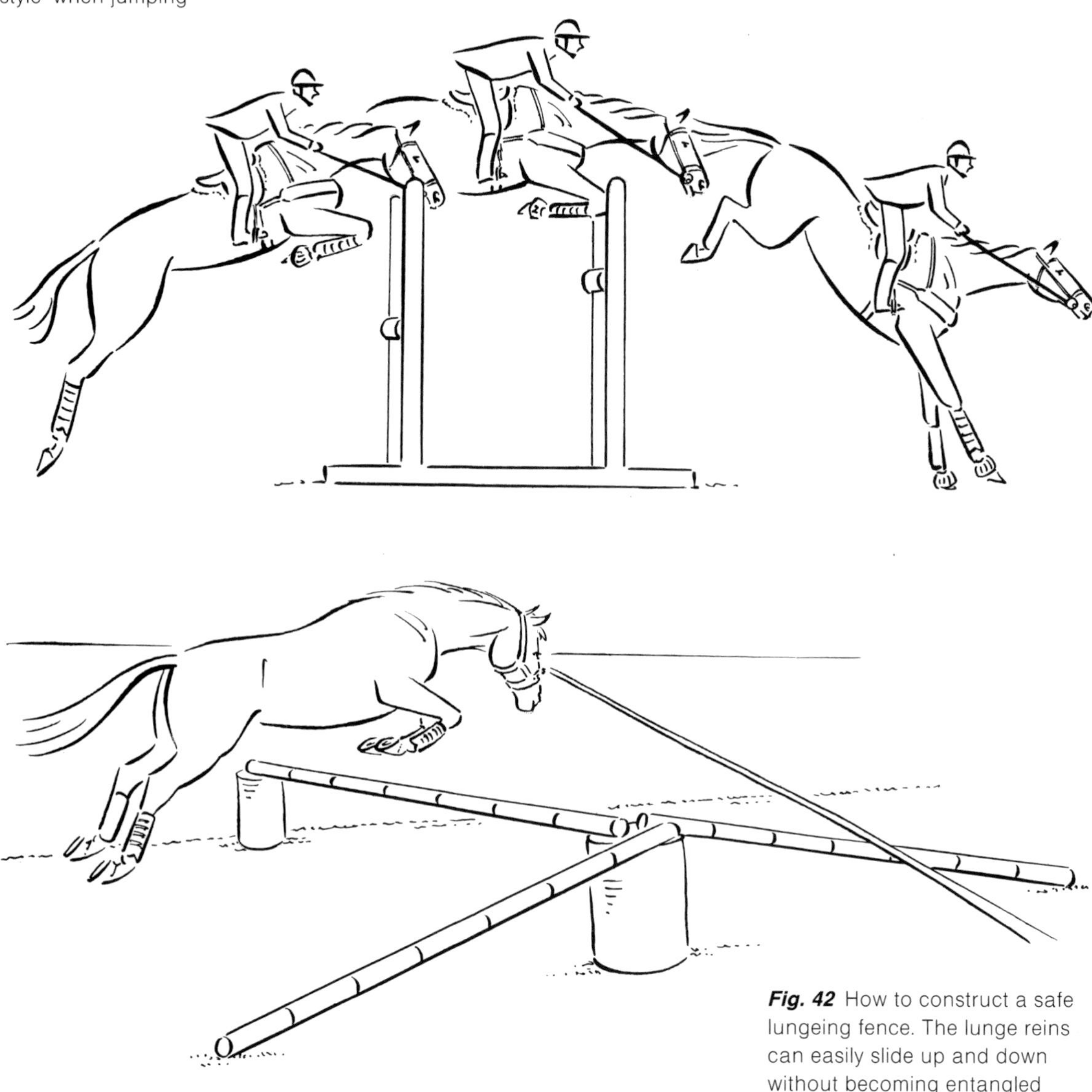

Fig. 42 How to construct a safe lungeing fence. The lunge reins can easily slide up and down without becoming entangled

ever attempting to do so with a youngster, and then you should only long rein from the cavesson and not the bit.

Long reining over fences can be beneficial for the horse which has a tendency to rush his fences, as the trainer has more control over the horse's pace. As when introducing the horse to long reining, the inside rein should come directly to the trainer's hand and not pass through the stirrup first.

Tack

The tack used for all forms of jumping from the ground is the same for as for each activity when jumping is not involved. Side reins are not used at any time, however, as this would restrict the horse through his neck and back. Stirrups which are left on the saddle while lungeing, prior to riding, should be well-secured **(fig. 43)**.

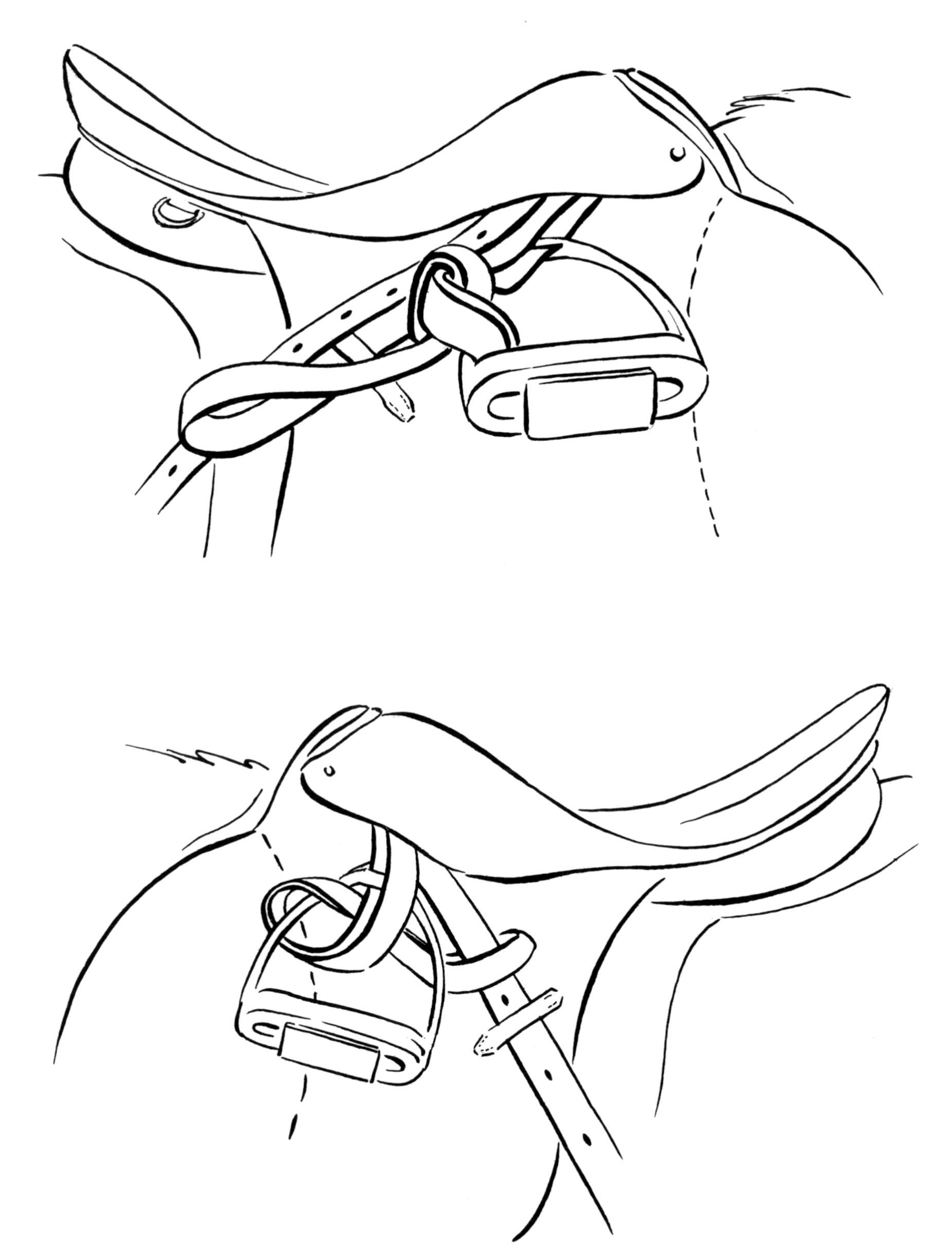

Fig. 43 Two methods of securing the stirrups when lungeing prior to riding

SAFETY CHECKLIST

At all times throughout the horse's training, you must ensure his and your own safety, even at the risk of halting progress. If things do go wrong and an accident occurs, the horse could be set back weeks or perhaps months. To ensure safety, always double-check certain points before proceeding. It is a good idea to have a mental checklist to tick off before each session, whether mounted or dismounted.

- Have I checked that the tack that I am using is in good repair?
- Have I checked that it is fitted correctly?
- Have I forgotten to fit any item?
- Am I wearing the necessary safety equipment: gloves, hard hat, etc?
- Have I checked the working area?
- Have I checked my horse's health?
- Have I really got the time for this session or will I have to rush?
- Can I manage to do this on my own?

The importance of experienced handlers

Although it is possible to learn how to carry out an activity if you really want to, it is important that you do not experiment with your youngster. You should at least have the knowledge of how to perform tasks, before trying to accomplish them, and then you would hopefully have the opportunity of gaining experience on an older, more experienced horse.

While the basic training of the young horse is within the scope of most people who wish to try it, the more advanced training that a horse requires in order to go into a particular sphere is best carried out under the guidance of an experienced trainer in the field. Always be aware of your abilities, and do not imagine that you have learned it all because you have produced your youngster to this stage.

The value of a good lungeing horse

The value of a good lungeing horse is two-fold. Firstly, the horse can be worked with ease if, for some reason, he is unable to be ridden, and, secondly, he can be an invaluable asset when teaching novices to ride.

The good lungeing horse is a special animal indeed. He needs to have an extremely calm temperament, and to obey the trainer whatever else is happening on his back. He needs to be fairly solid physically and fairly relaxed mentally, yet he also needs to be active and forward-going into the bargain. Such a horse, once found – or made – is therefore highly valued.

The youngster will not be useful as a lungeing horse for novices, and nor will the horse which is destined for greater things. The type of horse that is required is therefore likely to be over six years old, without the ability to go on to stardom in any field. Yet the horse which has proven unsound in training will not be an option either as he will not stand up to the very demanding work of the lungeing horse.

The horse which has been trained to lunge well is therefore always going to be of use. You should bear this in mind when training, as your youngster could even end up in this sphere.

Ending on a good note

Whenever you work a horse – whether mounted or dismounted – you should always have long- and short-term goals, from establishing a square halt for the first time, to taking part in your first competition. Whatever your goals, however, you should always aim to end on a good note, and to reward the horse accordingly.

You can always ensure that you do this by not asking for anything new or too demanding at the end of a session. The short-term goal for each session should be introduced in mid-session, and, if the horse achieves the goal, you can finish early and reward him well. If he does not achieve the goal for any session, you can resume an exercise already understood, and, once it is completed, you can still reward him well.

By following this policy, the horse will always end his sessions in a happy frame of mind, and will come out the next time ready to work for you as best he can. If you insist on the accomplishment of your goals, at all costs, you will dishearten the horse, and he will soon become sick and sorry. When he comes out again he will therefore not have the inclination to work well, and so will not make progress.

KEY POINTS

- Lungeing can play a large part in the further training of the horse, once he has been backed and ridden.
- All of the gaits, as well as upward and downward transitions, can be performed on the lunge.
- Most evasions occur through bad training, and not through the fault of the horse alone.
- One of the most common problems is overwork at too young an age, which strains muscles.
- Loose jumping teaches the horse to negotiate obstacles without hindrance, so that he learns to lengthen or shorten his stride as necessary on the approach.
- The idea of unridden jumping exercises is to get the horse to use himself to his best physical advantage.
- At all times throughout the horse's training, you must ensure his and your own safety, even at the risk of halting progress.
- You should follow established principles, and never experiment with the youngster.
- The good lungeing horse is a highly valued animal and will always be of use.
- Whenever you work a horse – whether mounted or dismounted – you should always have long- and short-term goals.
- Whatever your goals, you should always aim to end on a good note, and to reward the horse accordingly.

10

DESTINATIONS

As has been shown, the starting process and basic training for all horses – whatever, the sphere for which they are destined – is the same. If you think about this logically, it is obvious that, only when the horse has been schooled enough to demonstrate the abilities that he has, can you branch off into any specific area of training. As you cannot make judgements on the destination of any horse before he is started and ridden, it is impossible to set an individual training plan.

Training regimes for potential competition horses

If you have the desire to compete with your horse, you will now be looking to train him further for a specific job. This could be eventing or showing, for instance, and each area will make different demands on the horse, although there are training patterns common to all competition horses. The potential dressage horse will still benefit from jumping, while the build-up of a show jumper does not solely consist of jumping sessions, but also includes more advanced training on the flat, which will enhance his jumping.

You should therefore still hack your horse out, letting him experience all sorts of terrain, such as uneven ground and hills. This should be supported by work on the lunge and long reins, and even loose schooling and jumping.

The most important ingredient of any training regime is *variation*. When you consider this, you must not forget that this will include one rest day a week, in which the horse is turned out to do as he pleases. If you keep your horse interested in his work, you will then be able to carry out the training he may need for his chosen area of specialization.

Taking young horses on outings

It would be foolish to imagine that you could train your horse at home to a standard required for novice competitions, and then to take him out and expect him to behave impeccably. Horses are not machines, and need to be accustomed to the atmosphere that a show creates with its loudspeakers, spectators, flags and other horses. It is a good idea to take your horse to shows throughout the starting process, in order to allow him to become accustomed to them without the added pressure of having to perform **(73)**. This is also another way of including variation in your training process.

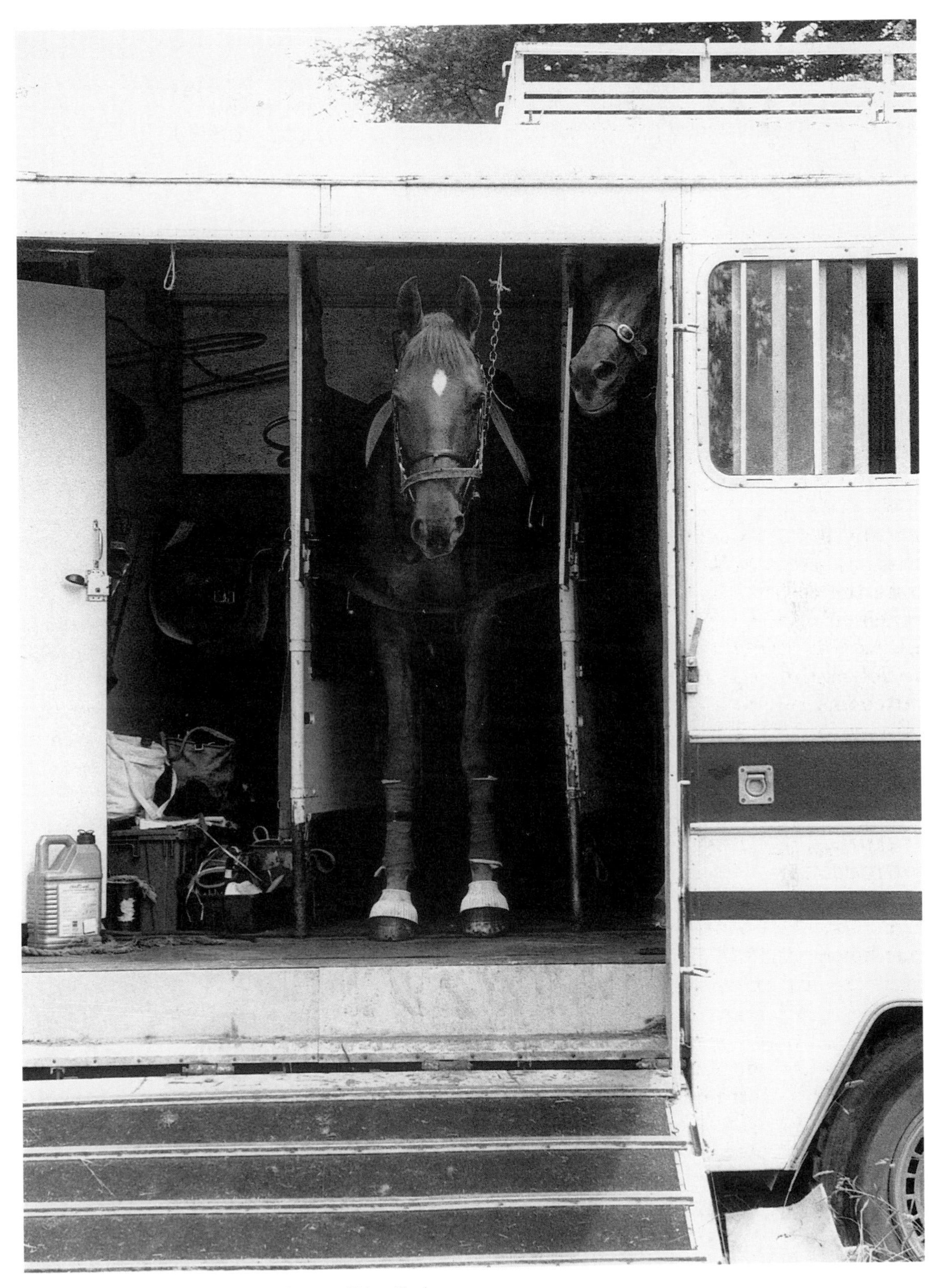

73 Taking the young horse to shows will familiarize him with all the new sights and sounds

WHAT TYPE OF HORSE DO YOU HAVE?

- **A genuinely enthusiastic character:** the most desirable young horse is one which has a genuinely enthusiastic outlook on life and is always happy in all that he does. He will have been easy to train and a pleasure to ride, and will always give you enjoyment. He may not be a great star, but he will always have a go at whatever you ask, and will be far more useful for the majority of riders than the potentially brilliant horse, which, after more years of effort spent in developing his ability, eventually falls short of the mark.
- **A bold horse:** a bold horse will give great enjoyment to a competitive rider, especially if the horse is a good jumper. Boldness can be encouraged if it is already within the horse's character, but it cannot be created. The horse should not, however, be encouraged to be so bold that he starts to take matters into his own hands and becomes bolshy. A bold horse therefore needs a rider who is strong and confident themselves.
- **A timid horse:** the timid horse is by nature a nervous character, and will take flight when faced with the unknown or difficult situations. Such horses can be calmed down by patient, caring handling, but they will never lose their nervousness completely, and are consequently unlikely to be suited to competitive work. The owner of such a horse will therefore need to accept these limitations, and should not be too competitively ambitious, or the horse will be a constant source of frustration.
- **A lazy horse:** a naturally lazy horse can drive his owner to distraction. Most are not hopeless cases, however, and can be improved by strict riding. A horse of this type is likely to suit an owner who likes to go out on long, safe hacks or who enjoys the occasional day's hunting.
- **A dangerous horse:** a truly dangerous horse is likely to have a mental problem of some kind. As there are very few truly dangerous horses, however, you need to ensure that the horse has not been abused or poorly trained, or that he is in pain, before you condemn him. This horse needs special handling, and should be passed to someone who has a good understanding of horse psychology. He is not a horse for the average rider to keep and persevere with in the hope of improvement. If the horse does have a mental defect, he will ultimately have to be humanely destroyed.

The aim is for the horse to produce the same standard of work at a show as he does at home. Without this essential pre-show training, this would be impossible to achieve.

Decisions – what next for the youngster?

Once the horse has established his natural rhythm and paces, you will be able to see whether he moves well enough in all paces to be a dressage horse **(fig. 44)**. As a horse should not be jumped until he has reached this level in his basic schooling, it is also only at this stage that you will see whether he has the ability to go on to become a show jumper **(fig. 45)**.

His physical make-up and mental attitude will also be deciding factors, and these are often not established until this stage. Although the horse may have tremendous jumping ability, it is going to be extremely difficult to develop and use this if his mental attitude is not stable. Some people are prepared to persevere with such an animal in the hope that his ability alone will carry him through, or that they will eventually discover the key to making use of that ability.

Once you have trained your horse, it is

Fig. 44 The potential dressage horse must possess athletic, elastic movement, as well as discipline and control

Fig. 45 The show jumper must possess different abilities, including physical strength and a jump which has plenty of scope

up to you to make the best of what you have, and you will have the task of deciding where his future lies. Most of us will be happy if we have managed to produce a horse which is sensible to ride and one with which we can have a bit of fun **(74)**. Some of us may be lucky enough to end up with a horse which shows great promise in one sphere or another, and hopefully one in which we are interested **(75)**.

The decision of what to do with your horse once you have trained him is a difficult one, especially if you have definite competitive aspirations and your horse has not lived up to expectation. There are many horses which do not suit one person, but are ideally suited to another. If you do find that you have a horse with which you feel sure you will not get on, you could of course always find the horse a new home, and start all over again **(76)**!

74 *(Left)* Many people who train a young horse will not have great competitive ambitions, but will be happy with a good all-rounder, which will always be a useful horse

75 *(Above)* Your horse may show great ability in a particular area

76 *(Right)* If you have enjoyed training your first horse, you may well wish to repeat the experience with a new foal

APPENDIX
A TRAINING SCHEDULE FOR YOUNG HORSES

What follows is only meant as a guide to the sort of timetable you can work towards with your young horse. It is very important that you always treat your horse as an individual and only progress at a rate with which his physical and mental development can cope.

At birth

Accustoming to your voice
Gentle stroking

From birth to weanling

Voice acceptance and recognition
Accepting the foaling slip
Acceptance of being stroked
Teaching not to pull away when foaling slip is held
Teaching to lead while following dam
Picking up feet in turn
Grooming with soft brush
Teaching to be caught along with dam
Showing in public with dam
Introduction to farrier
Introduction to hard feed
Introducing a worming and vaccination programme

From weanling to yearling

Weaned from dam at about six months of age provided youngster is eating well
Tying up without resistance
Stable manners
Recognition of key words
No resistance to general handling
No resistance to grooming
Respect for *any* handler
Standing still when required
Leading to and from playmates
Leading obediently anywhere you desire
Rollering if rugging up
Rugging up

From yearling to two-year old

Re-inforcing earlier lessons
Leading about the yard/farm
Leading on the roads
Bitting
Acceptance of being bathed, having mane/tail pulled
Castration of colts in spring
Showing in public
Loading into trailer
Trotting up in-hand
Standing squarely and still when halted

From two-year old to three-year old

Re-inforcing earlier lessons
Maintaining obedience
Showing
Rollering in preparation for backing if not already done

From three-year old to four-year old

Training to ride
Loose schooling
- introducing lungeing tack
- saddling

Lungeing
Long reining
- in the school
- away from the working area

Obedience when training
Backing
Walking whilst ridden on lunge
Trotting while ridden on lunge
Standing to be mounted
Acceptance of the legs
Turning away

From four-year old onwards

Re-backing
Acceptance of the aids
Hacking out
Establishing rhythm and correct paces
Executing transitions correctly
Progressive exercises
Working through
Work in canter
Developing fitness
Advanced training
- in-hand
- ridden

Jumping
- loose schooling
- lungeing
- long reigning
- ridden

Competitive spheres

BIBLIOGRAPHY

Crossley, Anthony *Dressage, The Seat, Aids and Exercises*
Edwards, Elwyn Hartley *Saddlery*
Goody, Peter *Horse Anatomy*
Hayes, Capt. M. Horace, FRCVS *Veterinary Notes for Horse Owners*
Oliver and Langrish *A Photographic Guide to Conformation*
Ross *School Exercises for Flatwork and Jumping*
Rossdale, Dr Peter MA, FRCVS *The Horse from Conception to Maturity*
Smythe, R. H., MRCVS and Goody, Dr P., B.Sc., Ph.D, revised by Gray, Peter MVB, MRCVS *Horse Structure and Movement*
Stainer, Sylvia *The Art of Long Reining*
Stainer, Sylvia *The Art of Lungeing*
Thelwall, Jane *The Less than Perfect Horse*
Williams, Moyra *Horse Psychology*

GLOSSARY

ACTION – the way in which a horse naturally moves.

AIDS –

natural – the seat, legs, voice and hands.

artificial – whips, spurs and martingales.

ASSOCIATION OF IDEAS – employing the horse's memory to relate to an experience or action with his own behaviour.

BACKING – the act of first mounting a horse.

BALANCE – an ability of the horse to carry himself and/or his rider without undue stress while maintaining his rhythm.

BENDING – where the horse is able to curve himself around a bend without turning his head or neck.

BITTING – the act of first putting a bit in the horse's mouth.

BONDING – intimacy and respect between horse and human.

BONE – the measurement taken all the way around the horse's lower leg just below the knee, denotes the 'amount of bone' that he has.

BOXING – the act of putting the horse into a horsebox or trailer.

BOXY FEET – small, enclosed, upright feet – a conformation fault.

BREAKING – training a horse to accept a rider and to be ridden – 'starting' is the preferred term for this book.

BREED – the type of horse; *Welsh, thoroughbred, Irish draught,* for example.

BRUSHING – where the insides of the pasterns/fetlocks rub together when the horse moves.

CANTER – a six-eight pace, between trot and gallop.

CASTRATING – removal of a male horse's testicles.

CAVALLETTI – poles attached to a cross of wood at each end which can be raised or lowered by simply rotating them.

CAVESSON – a piece of tack fitted to the horse's head which enables him to be lunged.

CHANGE OF LEG – where the horse changes his leading leg when in canter.

CHANGE OF REIN – to go the opposite way around the school, from being on the inside rein to the outside rein, or vice-versa.

CHARACTER – the horse's personality.

CIRCLES – ridden or performed in-hand to supple the horse.

COMPANIONS – other animals in the field, preferably of same age when youngsters.

CONDITION – nutritional state, how fat or thin the horse is – variable.

CONFORMATION – structural shape of the horse – permanent.

CONTACT – that which the horse seeks through the bit with the rider's hand.

CREEP FEEDING – feeding of the foal (excluding the dam) from about three weeks onwards.

CRIB-BITING – a vice where the horse takes hold of a solid object and sucks air.

DAM – mother of a foal.

DEVELOPMENT –

physical – the way in which the horse grows and matures.

mental – the way in which the horse copes with development and environmental change.

DISCIPLINE – teaching obedient behaviour.

DISHING – fault in action, where the horse throws one or both front feet out sideways when moving compared to breast-stroke in swimming).

DOUBLE – two fences of related distance, designed so that the horse takes a predefined number of strides between the two.

DRESSAGE – the art of training the horse to perform movements in a balanced and obedient manner.

EXERCISING – that which is carried out solely to keep the horse healthy as opposed to work which requires the horse to perform as requested.

FENCES –

enclosures – those which prevent a horse from escaping out of his paddock.

jumps – those which rider and trainer asks the horse to leap over.

FIGURE-OF-EIGHT – school movement where the horse follows the pattern of an 8.

FILLET STRING – a cord around the back edge of a rug which sits under the tail to prevent the rug from flapping up and back over the horse.

FLIGHT REFLEX – instant reaction to flee from something frightening.

FOAL – a young horse from birth to six months of age.

FOREHAND – where the horse carries most of his weight on his front legs.

FORGEING – where the horse hits one shoe with the other.

FREEZE MARK – identifying mark branded onto a horse.

GADGETS – useful training aids.

GALLOP – fastest pace of the horse.

GASKIN – the horse's second thigh, located on the upper hind leg.

HALF-HALT – asking the horse for halt but moving him on again before it is fully executed, creates impulsion.

HAND – measurement of horses; 1 hand equals 4 ins.

HEAD-CARRIAGE – the way the horse holds his head and arches his neck to varying degrees depending on level of schooling.

HOMEBRED – horse bred to keep and train rather than as a commercial proposition.

IMPULSION – energy generated by the rider through the horse, which enables him to perform as required.

IN-HAND – any activity without a rider.

KEY WORDS – words which once understood by the horse allow you to manoeuvre him without confusion.

KICKING – natural defence of the horse which must be repressed around humans.

LAMENESS – where the horse is not sound on any leg due to injury or disease.

LATERAL WORK – moving sideways as well as forwards and backwards.

LONG-REINING – in-hand schooling using two reins, where the horse can be asked to move wherever the trainer so desires.

LOOSE SCHOOLING – where the horse is completely loose within the school, but still under the guidance of the trainer.

LUNGEING – in-hand schooling where the horse is required to work on a circle around the trainer.

MOUTHING – encouraging the horse to accept a contact between the bit in his mouth and pressure on the other end of the reins.

NAPPING – refusal of the horse to go where the rider or trainer asks – pulling towards the gate for home.

OVERBENT – where the horse tips his head inwards towards his chest and so loses contact with the bit.

OVERFACED – where the horse has been asked to do something for which he is either incapable or not ready.

OVERREACH BOOT – a rubber boot in the shape of a 'bell' which fits over the horse's hoof and bulbs of the heel.

PACES – walk, trot, canter and gallop, and collection and extension with each.

PARROT-MOUTHED – where the upper jaw overshoots the lower jaw.

PERFORMANCE HORSE – horse which competes at high level in a given sphere.

REIN-BACK – movement of stepping back a few paces when asked.

RESCHOOLING – schooling the horse again if bad habits have been allowed to develop.

RESISTANCE – reluctance of the horse to perform as asked.

RHYTHM – even hoofbeats at any pace requested and through transitions – 'keeping the rhythm'.

ROLLERING – the act of putting on the roller/training surcingle for the first time, prior to saddling and riding.

SCHOOLING – exercises and paces dictated by the rider under controlled conditions to improve the horse's way of going.

SERPENTINES – even loops back and forth across the school.

SIDE REINS – short reins which run from bit to saddle during lungeing.

SOUNDNESS – without lameness or defect in health.

STAMP – the build of the horse.

STARTING – the process through which the horse is trained to be ridden.

SUPPLING – achieved through exercises and transitions which enable the horse to move more freely and in balance.

TEETHING – period during which the young horse's teeth are erupting through the gums.

TEMPERAMENT – the horse's disposition – may be kind or grumpy, for instance.

THICK-SET – broad under the jaw and down the neck – conformation fault.

TRAFFIC PROOF – does not misbehave in any form of traffic.

TRANSITIONS – the period from one pace to the next, may be upward – from walk to trot, or downward – from canter to trot, for example.

UNSPOILED – a horse which has not had someone attempt to train him and failed.

VETTING – having the veterinary surgeon give an opinion of the horse's soundness and suitability before purchase.

VICES – bad habits such as weaving or crib biting, or undesirable behaviour such as bucking or rearing.

WEANLING – horse from six months to one year old.

WEANING – the act of separating the foal from its dam.

WEAVING – a vice where the horse steps from one foot to the other behind the stable door and rocks back and forth with his head and neck.

WORKING AREA – the place where the horse is trained or schooled.

YOUNGSTER – a horse up until about the age of five where he is learning things for the first time.

YEARLING – a horse from one up until two years of age.

INDEX